WITHDRAWN

E.G. Melroe   1892-1955

*"He was the best boss
who ever hired a man!"*

Ted Melroe

"E.G."
Inventor
By Necessity

The Story of E. G. Melroe
and The Melroe Company

By Robert F. Karolevitz

203069

HD
9486
.U6
M45

Library of Congress catalog card number 68-57105
Manufactured in the United States of America
Second Edition, October 1968

Copyright © 1968 by

NORTH PLAINS PRESS
ABERDEEN, S. DAK.

To Mabel Melroe

who, in her own quiet way,
was the heroine of this story.

Forward

The small towns of rural America are not doomed—at least as long as there are imaginative, industrious, indomitable people like the Melroes of Gwinner, North Dakota.

Gwinner is a most illogical setting for a multi-million dollar success story. By almost every appropriate measuring stick, the tiny hamlet in Sargent County has no business being the industrial capital of North Dakota.

And yet it is!

Because E. G. Melroe had equal endowments of inventive genius and Norwegian tenacity, he developed an idea into a machine and a machine into a manufacturing company. As a result, a dying prairie village shucked its funereal crepe paper and became a vibrant, happy town again.

To most non-farmers, the original Melroe products—a combine pickup and a spring-tooth harrow—are neither romantic nor, for that matter, recognizable. Still, they filled an important need for agriculturists and were instrumental in reversing Gwinner's downhill slide toward historical oblivion.

This book was compiled more than a dozen years after E. G.'s death, and since he left no personally written memoirs of his activities, the recollections about him and his work have had to come from those who knew him first-hand during his fruitful life in Bowen Township. Even in that short time, though, memories have a way of dropping nuances or adding embellishments so that there is a danger of inaccurate portrayal. In the relating of certain minor events, for instance, three different versions came from three different people, each of whom insisted that he alone was right. Wherever possible, such multiple interpretations were checked and rechecked until a single, most reasonable viewpoint evolved.

The result, hopefully, is E. G. Melroe as he was, as he worked and as he dreamed. There is hope, too, that this small volume might muffle the bleatings of those social theorists who preach the demise of the small communities of back-track America. E. G. proved that it is possible to jump the traces of industrial convention and still succeed. In that regard he may well be a notable pioneer in the decentralization of factories and the revival of other potential ghost towns like Gwinner.

No wonder North Dakota is proud of the farmer-inventor of Sargent County and the family enterprise he created!

Robert F. Karolevitz

A Table of Contents

(Above) The farm Mollerud, in center of photo, was the originating site of the
Melroe story. It still exists in the Solor district of the province of Hedmark in
Norway. (Below) The farm Mollerud as it appeared in 1935.

Chapter 1

The Strength of Scandinavia

Some 80 miles north of Oslo, Norway, is an ancient farm bearing the name Mollerud. For generations it had been the property of the Lundeby family, and in 1835 when young Gunder Reierson Lundeby married and moved to the ancestral site, he adopted its name as his own.

Gunder Mollerud and Maren Tostensdatter Vold, his bride, thus prepared to establish a new line of hardy, purposeful Norwegians who—they envisioned—would carry on the traditions of their namesake estate. In the region of Solor, Gunder was known for his athletic agility and physical strength. He also had great interest in and knowledge of the forests of the district, and he invested in timberlands and used his brawn to harvest the trees and ship them to market in Christiania, as Oslo was then called.

11

One winter day, according to family legend, Gunder and a relative were traveling across a frozen lake, each in a light sleigh pulled by a single horse. All of a sudden the ice gave way beneath them, and—as the men leaped to safety—both horses plunged into the frigid water. With no fear for his own life, Gunder grabbed for his horse's bridle, and "with the power of ten men" pulled the animal and sleigh out of the lake. He then went back and got the second horse.

On another occasion, when he was traveling by sleigh to Christiania on business, he was attacked by a pair of robbers. After he had physically thrown one of his would-be assailants into a snowbank, the other fled in terror, and Gunder calmly continued his journey.

The diligent young timber entrepreneur and his wife had three daughters and four sons, and life at the farm Mollerud was cheerful, productive and promising. Then, in the late summer of 1855, the 36-year-old father found it necessary to make another trip to the capital city in behalf of his enterprise. This time he hitched his horse to a *karjol*, a light two-wheeled cart used for speedy travel. His primary mission was to collect for a shipment of trees, so the journey down the beautiful Glomma River valley promised to be a pleasant one. It was, instead, to be unexpectedly tragic.

When he had completed his business transactions, Gunder started the long trip home. As he neared the village of Kongsvinger, he suddenly became ill. There was a doctor in the town, but in those still-groping days of medicine, the physician could do little to help. On the 21st of September Gunder Mollerud died, a victim of an undetermined abdominal ailment.

For more than a century his strange death has been the subject of controversy. Supposedly, when the bereaved widow arrived to claim his body, she found no money for the timber payment. Still later, Maren Mollerud lost the timberland in what family genealogists have called "a questionable legal maneuver."

At the time of her husband's death, the widow's children ranged from Randine, a 14-year-old daughter, to the infant Gunnar born earlier in 1855. Also sharing the grief were Theodor, 12; Didrik, 10; Marthe, 8; Oluf, 6, and Lovise, 3. Somehow through the years she managed to raise each of them to adulthood, but the dreams she and Gunder had so jubilantly fashioned crashed and shattered on that fateful September day in Kongsvinger. (Maren herself lived to be 101 years old at the time of her death on April 28, 1921. Her seven children were equally long-lived, having an average life-span of exactly 80 years.)

As her family matured, Maren was tormented by the persistent rumor that Gunder had been poisoned. The children heard it, too, and couldn't help but be influenced by the connotations, especially when the farm forests were no longer theirs. Particularly affected were the four brothers. Farmland in Norway was growing less available with each generation, and therefore the matter of livelihood became a problem of serious concern.

In America, meanwhile, the scars of the Civil War were beginning to heal, at least superficially, and the opening of the vast new frontiers of the West had begun. Railroads crossed the Mississippi River and edged onto the expansive prairies; land was available in almost unlimited quantities, and the news of this potential opportunity created an excitement among the young men of Norway as it did elsewhere in land-hungry Europe. Agents of the railroad companies and boomer towns crossed the Atlantic to distribute folders and to tack up posters which promised a bright, prosperous future in the New World. Two of the Mollerud brothers, already in their thirties and with little hope of other than meager existence in Norway, began to think seriously of emigration.

The first was Didrik, third eldest of the children, who saw in the United States an answer to his personal dilemma. Like thousands of other hopeful young Norwegians, he made the fateful decision and embarked for America. This

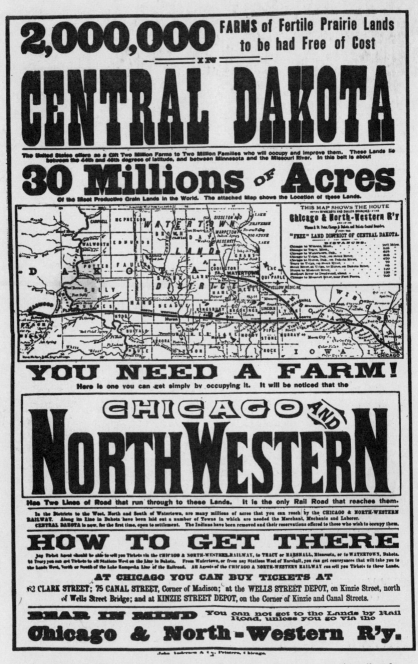

Free land for homesteaders was the clarion call sent out by the railroads in the seventies and early eighties. Posters were put up everywhere, even in Europe, for the land-hungry to read and heed.

was at the time when the Dakota Central division of the Chicago and North Western Railway was extending beyond its earlier terminus at Canby, Minnesota, toward the new town of Huron, Dakota Territory. Didrik Mollerud, with many of his countrymen, was lured by the C&NW's promise of "2,000,000 farms of fertile prairie lands to be had free of cost," and ultimately he arrived at De Smet, one of several exuberant young hamlets on the railroad line. Apparently it was Didrik, who like other Norse immigrants, was concerned about the spelling and pronunciation of his family name. In America he found that the non-Scandinavian people with whom he dealt—especially the always-in-a-hurry governmental agents—seemed to have particular trouble with the umlaut over the "o." So, to solve the problem the Mollerud, which had once been Lundeby, was changed to the more Americanized Melroe.

Didrik, meanwhile, maintained contact with his younger brother, Oluf, who was also anxious to come to the United States. The latter was a journeyman carpenter, a skill which was to prove of great value to him when he, too, arrived in De Smet, eager to acquire a farm of his own. Following Didrik's lead, he also changed his name to Melroe.

The treeless expanse of the Dakota Territory momentarily stunned Oluf Melroe, as it did countless other Norwegians who were accustomed to the forests, fjords and the irregular beauty of their homeland. Still, the almost flat, almost barren prairie offered unlimited opportunity for any young man who would accept the challenge of 160 virgin acres on the public domain according to the requirements of the Homestead Act of May 20, 1862.

When Oluf arrived in Kingsbury County and made contact with Didrik, he immediately began to search for land. Wherever he went, he tested the earth with a shovel, because with 30,000,000 acres to choose from (according to the railroad poster), he wanted to make sure he got good land. In his estimation, the soil around De Smet was dry and had a hardpan crust beneath it. Consequently, he decided to look elsewhere.

Somewhere in his meanderings, Oluf met Ole and Lars E. (Louie) Halin, brothers from Sweden who also happened to be carpenters. In their first years in America, they were no doubt grateful for one another's company, and apparently they planned their future moves together, too. While none of the three left a diary or detailed chronology of their activities at that time, they presumably shared a desire for homestead land, and when the Northern Pacific Railroad began to stretch its line westward into what was eventually to become Sargent County, North Dakota, the immigrant partners decided to take a first-hand look at the new territory. Louie and Oluf (and possibly Ole) went to Tower City, North Dakota, rented a cart and horse and drove southward to the region between the Wild Rice and Sheyenne Rivers where many other Swedes and Norwegians were settling. Again Oluf's shovel tested the land, and this time he found soil which satisfied him. He promptly filed his claim on the Northwest Quarter of Section 8, in Township 131 North, of Range 56 West, of the Fifth Principal Meridian in Dakota Territory. The year was 1882, and the 34-year-old Norse carpenter had at last found the "freedom soil" he craved. Louie Halin filed nearby, and later Ole bought a neighboring homestead.

Buffalo bones were everywhere, giving the impression that an old civilization had died and a new one was about to be born. That was Oluf's feeling exactly as he started to erect the first crude dwelling on his own land. Even a craftsman could not build without good lumber, though, so for a time he had to be satisfied with a temporary clapboard shanty. The Northern Pacific's nearest terminus was at Linton (first called "End of the Line" and then "Graball") some 16 miles northeast of the Melroe claim. By September 6, 1883, when Sargent County was officially organized, the townsite had been moved three miles westward and renamed Milnor—but Oluf had dreams to dream and sod to break so he had little time to concern himself with the problems of governmental organization, even though he probably would have enjoyed the heated arguments and near-fisticuffs at the political meeting called at Lake Kandiotta eleven miles east of his claim to establish a county seat.

His neighbors in Bowen Township (named for the parents of Ed W. Bowen, one of the earliest homesteaders) included A. M. Cook, L. E. Halin, Gust Edman, Gust Anderson and Andrew Wahlund, Sr. They lived in a variety of tar-paper shacks, sod houses and dugouts, and like Oluf Melroe, they looked for better days ahead.

It was Oluf's plan not to live permanently on his claim until he was married, so throughout the good-weather months, he fulfilled the requirements of the Homestead Act. Then he left the township to find winter employment which provided him with the capital he needed for developing his land. He worked for a time in a grocery store in Harlem, and with the Halin brothers, he built railroad cars in Brainerd, Minnesota. One winter he and the Halins hired out as carpenters to help on the construction of the West Hotel in Minneapolis. In later years he always enjoyed relating an anecdote of that particular employment.

Oluf, it seems, was one of four carpenters assigned to lay a very fine hardwood floor. One of the men, however, was a Scandinavian snoose-chewer who promiscuously spat tobacco juice on the completed work, discoloring the light-hued oak boards with brownish blotches. The boss came by, looked around and then asked one of the workers for a bite of his tobacco plug.

"I'm sorry," said the man, "but I don't chew."

The boss then asked Oluf and got the same reply. Whereupon the carpenter who had been doing the splattering heard the boss's request and, thinking he might make some points for himself, whipped out his plug and offered it to the overseer with a flourish. That was all the evidence the foreman needed, and he promptly sent the culprit packing, to the delight of Oluf and his partners who were not particularly happy about the use of their handiwork as a giant spittoon.

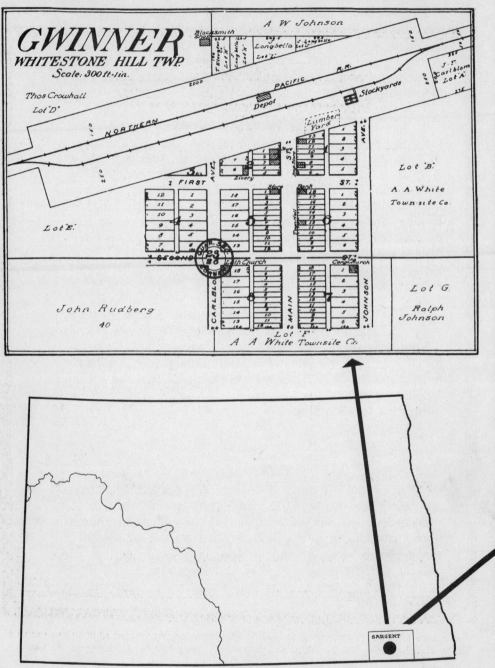

NORTH DAKOTA

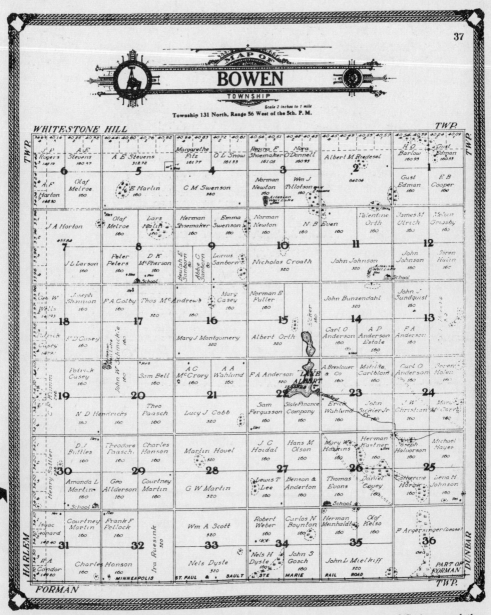

These maps from an atlas printed in the early 1900's show the original platting of Gwinner and the locations of the various homesteads in Bowen Township. Misspelled names were quite common.

Among the newcomers to Sargent County was Miss Kari
Ellefson from Nes, Hallingdal, in Norway. She had been
born on November 19, 1862, and was in her early twenties
when Oluf Melroe met her. Kari had been working in
Milnor, among other things as a cook in the hotel. Despite
the difference in their ages, he courted her, and on
November 28, 1886, she became his bride. He was almost
37 years old; she had just turned 24. Together they tackled
the formidable task of proving up a claim on unbroken soil.
Already the northern portion of Dakota Territory was
becoming recognized as an ideal wheatland, with climatic
conditions and the soil of the gently rolling prairies highly
suitable to the production of "No. 1 hard." Still, with a
walking plow pulled by oxen or horses, it was not possible
for a homesteader to put in more than 10 or 15 new acres
in a year. If grasshoppers or drouth took the tiny crop, the
margin of survival was slim. Most settlers had a cow or two
to provide milk and cheese; some had a few sheep, and the
pioneer women carded and spun their own wool to make
mittens, caps and stockings for the harsh winters. Coal was
prohibitively expensive, and wood was scarce. Occasionally
the men would take a wagon to the Sheyenne or Wild Rice
Rivers to bring back a load of driftwood or logs of ash,
boxelder, willow or elm. When the wood was gone, the
settlers burned twisted prairie hay or buffalo chips gathered
around historic wallows.

Even after they were slaughtered to the brink of extinction, buffaloes (nobody called them bison) also provided
badly needed cash for the earliest homesteaders. They
gathered the bleached bones which were in demand by the
sugar refiners, chinaware manufacturers and fertilizer companies in the east. Luxuries of any kind were rare. Much of
the furniture was homemade and somewhat primitive. Kerosene lamps smelled up the tiny rooms and offered the
barest minimum of night-time lighting. Ingenuity and in-
ventiveness often accounted for what differences there were
in the levels of existence between one pioneer family and
another. The fact that Oluf was a good carpenter not only

gave the Melroes an advantage on their own farm, but he also hired out to build barns and houses for his neighbors when lumber became more available.

Oluf Melroe

Lars E. Halin (third from right) shared the rigors of homesteading with Oluf Melroe. This graphic photo, taken in the early 1900's, included (left to right): Tillie Melroe, Edwin Halin, Gina Melroe, Ella Halin, unidentified, L. E. Halin, Oscar Melroe and Ed Melroe.

Ed Melroe (arrow) attended Bowen School No. 1 for eight years, though he never quite completed the final grade. His brother Oscar posed at E. G.'s right.

In 1887, when both the Soo Line and Great Northern railways brought further development to Sargent County, Oluf and Kari also added to their family. Their first daughter, Mathilde, was born that year, to be followed by Gina in 1890, the second happy event of that twelve-month period. Earlier, on January 8 at the Land Office in Fargo, Oluf received Homestead Certificate No. 4285, attesting

that his hard-won 160 acres were granted to him, his heirs and assigns by the United States in the name of President Benjamin Harrison "to have and to hold. . . forever." Two years later, on April 23, their first son, Edward Gideon, was born.

Chapter 2

Monkey Wrenches, Baseball Bats and a Wedding Ring

In his earliest years Ed Melroe gave no indication of being a particularly unusual individual. He was, as a matter of fact, a typical, robust North Dakota farm boy, not at all unlike his equally typical brothers: Oscar, born in 1895; Sigurd, in 1899, and Theodore, in 1902.

Oluf and Kari had weathered the difficult years of proving up, a process which often consisted simply of stolid resistance to the ravages of nature. They had withstood blizzards, grasshopper plagues, crop-destroying hailstorms and disastrous drouth. Hundreds of less dogged homesteaders had knuckled under and deserted their claims, but the Melroes—strong-willed and hardy—had persisted and

25

won. The Panic of 1893 was a further test of their
tenacity; so was the loss of a new-born son (also named
Oscar) in 1894. If Ed Melroe inherited any outstanding
trait from his parents, it was this obdurate resolve to see a
job through.

Just before the turn of the century, Ed joined his sisters
at Bowen School No. 1. It was single-room frame structure,
heated by a fuel-gobbling stove to which the youngsters
had to haul seemingly endless arm loads of wood. In the
classroom Ed Melroe did not exhibit any notable preco-
cious development, though he did show considerable ability
in arithmetic, art and penmanship. He got into a normal
amount of mischief, threw a few spit wads and stayed after
school to dust the blackboard erasers for teasing the girls.

His most effective teacher, however, was his father, the
farmer-carpenter who taught a special life-long course in
common sense. From Oluf, Ed learned about the use and
care of tools. He grew up in an era of hand-labor;
consequently, it was impressed upon him quickly that a
sharp saw cut easier than a dull one, a simple but practical
axiom which he, in turn, would pass on to his own sons in
later years. With his brothers, he learned how to handle
multiple teams of horses, how to make temporary field
repairs with bits of wire and other expedients, how to
grease a wagon wheel and rivet broken harness. He learned,
too, how to plow a straight furrow, when to plant the
bountiful durum and what to do when a seeder clogged or
a sickle bar came out second best in an encounter with a
glacial rock. He was, like so many others of his generation,
schooled primarily in the simple practicalities of existence
on a horse-dominated North Dakota farm.

A new age was dawning, however. A year after Ed
Melroe was born, Charles E. and J. Frank Duryea were
unveiling what has generally been recognized as America's
first practical gasoline auto. In 1896, when Ed was four,
Henry Ford knocked part of a wall out of a brick
workshop so he could wheel his first Quadricycle onto the

A car salesman brought this Model T Ford out to the Melroe farm, but Oluf didn't buy. Instead, he and his family took advantage of the opportunity to be photographed. Left to right were Oluf, Kari, Gina, Ted, Ed, Sig and Oscar.

streets of Detroit. The horseless carriage became a reality
and by an accident of history, Ed's own life paralleled the
development of the automobile.

Even before he saw his first motor car, he had shown an
interest in what mechanical equipment his father had
acquired. Steam tractors fascinated him; so did reapers and
threshing machines. A propensity for tinkering began to
exert itself even before he left Bowen School No. 1
without finishing the eighth grade.

At that time, the farm youngster who went on to high
school was an exception to normal custom. There was then
no such facility in Gwinner, a tiny hamlet (some 6½ miles
northeast of the Melroe homestead) which had been established in 1900 when the Northern Pacific extended its line
westward from Milnor to Oakes. Then-thriving Harlem, the
northerly terminus of a Chicago, Milwaukee & St. Paul
Railroad spur (a few miles west of Oluf's claim), was also
without a secondary school. So Ed Melroe's formal educa-
tion was simply considered at an end and his career as a
North Dakota farmer begun.

By this time, of course, it was becoming obvious that the
internal combustion engine would be the automotive power
of the future. To Oluf's credit, he recognized his eldest
son's inclination towards things mechanical and arranged
for him to attend a special course in the rudiments of
steam and gas engines at the North Dakota Agricultural
College in Fargo. Later Ed completed a month-long auto
mechanics workshop in Omaha, Nebraska. Without knowing
it, he was laying the foundation for a life's role which
would ultimately affect the economy of his own community as well as that of North Dakota itself. On November 2,
1915, he signed up for a winter session at the Dakota
Business College in Fargo to pursue a concentrated curricu-
lum in bookkeeping, business mathematics, vocabulary
building, commercial law and penmanship. Years later they
remembered him at the school as a young man who wasn't
interested in simple, sterile answers; he always wanted to
know "why?"

Ed Melroe (left) at 20 with close friend Harry Spaulding.

Ed Melroe (left) posed in an observation car mock-up during his one-month stay in Omaha to study auto mechanics.

Meanwhile, there was a continuing schedule of farm work to do—on the original homestead, an adjacent 160-acre preemption claim and other land acquired or rented by the elder Melroe. For diversion, the boys hunted ducks and geese on the numerous sloughs in central Sargent County; they chased foxes on horseback; or they trapped muskrats, badgers, skunks, mink and other animals which flourished in the area. When Oluf bought his first automobile in 1914—a Maxwell touring car—his sons were overjoyed. Occasionally they "borrowed" it, by pushing it silently out of the farmyard and far enough down the road so their father wouldn't hear them start the engine.

There was seriousness and hi-jinks; big Sunday dinners with relatives and friends; Saturday nights in Harlem,

Gwinner and—on special occasions—in the county seat town
of Forman; numberless sessions of Norwegian whist; and
Old Country Christmas feeds of lutefisk and lefse. The
youngsters experienced some of the hardships of prairie
farming, too, and during one particularly bad snowstorm,
Ed Melroe—then a teen-ager—saddled a horse and rode out
into the blizzard in search of a flock of sheep which had
strayed from neighbor Albert E. Stevens' farm. He found
them two miles away, rounded up the near-frozen animals,
and managed to get 150 of them safely back to shelter.
Neighboring, he learned, was an important—almost vital—
necessity to the somewhat isolated farmers of North Dakota.

If Ed Melroe had a secondary interest besides mechanics,
it was baseball. He and his brothers loved the game, and

The 1914 Gwinner Giants (left to right): Blake Bishop, manager; unidentified,
but possibly a "borrowed" or hired player; Carl Peterson; Albin Carlblom;
Floyd (Hap) Hagedorn; Alex Mason; Alfred Hanson; Ed Melroe; Oscar Melroe;
John Ash and Oluf Nelson.

they were aided and abetted by Oluf, their number one
fan. The latter usually had farm chores assigned to the boys
on game days, but when it came time to leave, he always
relented, and quite often he climbed into the wagon and
rode along with the team. While they were of playing age,
there were always one or more Melroes on the Gwinner

town team, and they knew how to handle themselves on the diamond. *The Prairie Press* of Gwinner on April 29, 1915, carried the following front-page story:

> Gwinner fandom was treated to one of the cleanest ball games last Sunday on the local grounds it has had the pleasure of witnessing for many a moon. The locals appeared in their new uniforms, and a better looking bunch of ball players it is hard to conceive of. Despite the fact that little or no practice had been indulged in, each player appeared to be in fine trim, which was proven by the fact that the score stood 9 to 3 in favor of the Gwinner nine at the close of the ninth inning.

Farther down in the midst of the laudatory prose, the reporter finally got around to identifying the opposition as the neighboring town of Forman and to add:

> Ed and Oscar Melroe both participated in the game, playing left field and shortstop, respectively. The Melroe boys are heavy hitters and sure players and probably as good if not a little better than any others in the county. A ball batted towards a Melroe amounts to that much wasted effort on the batter's part as for the Melroe boys to miss is history.

A few years later Sig and Ted also joined their brothers on the team, and some of the Sargent County old-timers have speculated that Sigurd was the best of them all. He threw so hard, they reminisced, that he could field a ground ball in left field and still throw out a runner going into first base. No doubt the Melroe speed and ability came from the bloodlines of the powerful, athletic Gunder Mollerud; strengthened, most likely, by the physical heritage from Kari Ellefson's ancestors, the fabled high-kickers of Hallingdal.

Five miles from the Melroe homestead, over the line in White Stone Hill Township, lived the Nils Petterson family. (The name originally had just one "t," but it was changed to avoid confusion with that of another Nils Peterson on

The family homes of Oluf Melroe (top) and Nils Petterson (bottom) were built on the respective homestead sites soon after the turn of the century. Sunday dinners and holiday celebrations, with both Petterson and Melroe clans involved, were commonplace at each location.

The Petterson family, left to right: Laurence, Henry, Oscar, Ivar, parents Nils and Selma, Alma, Esther, Mabel and Myrtle.

In the first decade of the 1900's, the elder Melroes posed with their family. Left to right, front row: Oscar, Oluf, Ted, Kari and Sig; back row: Ed, Gina, Ivar Petterson and Tillie. The latter two were the first of the Petterson-Melroe intermarriages.

the same mail route.) Nils came from Skona, Sweden, where he had been born on October 29, 1856. In the spring of 1879 he arrived in Cakato, Minnesota, west of Minneapolis, where he remained for about two years before moving westward to become one of the earliest settlers in the Gwinner vicinity. He was an exuberant, ambitious young man who became a successful farmer and a winning politician on the local and state scenes. In the latter role, he had a most effective technique of communicating with individual constituents; he'd meet a man on the street, seize his hand and hold it firmly with a cow-milker's grip until he'd had his entire say. His listener simply couldn't escape. As a county commissioner, state representative and state senator, he was a most persuasive individual.

His wife, Selma Swanson, had been born in Stockholm and was brought to the United States as a child. She and Nils were the township's first newlyweds, traveling by horse and wagon to Lisbon, with Ole F. Johnson and Fred Carlblom—two other pioneer homesteaders—accompanying them as witnesses. After Judge E. J. Ryman had performed the ceremony, the couple returned the same day to their two-room shanty southwest of Gwinner to begin a long-term, fruitful partnership. Together they cut sod blocks to build a barn, and when Ivar, the first of their eight children arrived on January 1, 1884, Nils built Selma a cradle out of a 4-X coffee box.

One of the Petterson youngsters was a daughter, Mabel Florence, born on August 14, 1897. With her parents, she attended the occasional social events of the community and visited the neighbors, frequently for a table-warping Sunday dinner. The Nils Pettersons and Oluf Melroes were particular friends, so the families were often together at one home or the other. While the men argued politics or played whist and the women cooked and chatted, the children cavorted, played, teased and tussled. In the process, a natural affinity began to develop among the youngsters, a relationship which was to result in a somewhat unusual inter-family amalgam in future years.

As he grew up, when Ed Melroe wasn't thinking of motors, machinery or baseball, he thought about Mabel Petterson. (It was a friendly rivalry she would have to contend with for almost four decades.) Mabel attended school in Gwinner, and when she was 14, she became the organist in the Gustaf Adolf Lutheran Church of which her parents and the Oluf Melroes were charter members. Mabel also played piano in a local orchestra which provided music for dances in the nearby towns of Gwinner, Forman and Stirum, not to mention a few neighborhood barns like that of Alvin Lund which was swept and decorated for an occasional shindig.

Gustaf Adolf Lutheran Church.

While she fingered the melodies to such vintage tunes as
"Dreamland" and "Let Me Call You Sweetheart," Ed
Melroe would be on the dance floor, high-stepping it with
all the other pretty girls of Sargent County. To make sure
that the competition didn't get too keen, however, Mabel
would signal Florence Carlblom to substitute for her at the
piano while she enjoyed an occasional fox trot or a waltz
with her husky and handsome young beau. After the dance,
Ed would usually drive her home in his three-seated
"cloverleaf" Briscoe.

Her piano-playing obviously didn't interfere with ro-
mance any more than did Ed's penchant for mechanics,
because on March 14, 1917, they were married in the
Petterson family home, with Rev. Edor Larson of the
Gustaf Adolf Church officiating. Edward Melroe, the
sure-fielding baseball star of the Gwinner Giants, made one
of his rare errors: he dropped the ring at the crucial
moment and it rolled under the sofa. Brother Oscar re-
trieved it, though, and after a brief flush of embarrassment,
the ceremony resumed and Ed Melroe and Mabel Petterson
became man and wife.

Mr. and Mrs. Nils Petterson

announce the marriage of their daughter

Mabel Florence

to

Edward G. Melroe

on Wednesday, March fourteenth

one thousand nine hundred seventeen

Gwinner, North Dakota

At home
after April 1st
Cogswell, N. D.

Ed and Mabel Melroe posed for their wedding picture in 1917.

Chapter 3

An Inkling of Genius

Ed Melroe's life was one of practical consideration, so it was not unusual that his honeymoon should include a secondary mission. Andrew Ellefson, his mother's brother, was incurably ill in western North Dakota, and Ed was assigned the responsibility of disposing his uncle's property.

Oluf hitched a team and drove the newlyweds to the railroad station at Harlem, which, in a matter of a few short years, was to become a prairie ghost town when the Chicago, Milwaukee & St. Paul Railroad abandoned its spur line. In 1917, though, the rail terminus was very much alive when Ed and Mabel arrived to board the train to New England in the butte country of Hettinger County.

From New England they traveled by horse and wagon to the Ellefson claim where they finally found the ramshackle

41

shanty which was to be their honeymoon cottage. It was not at all the romantic setting a young woman dreams about, and Ed soon moved his bride in with neighbors while he completed his family obligation. It was, the Melroes concluded, an ideal place to start a marriage; from there, the only direction to go was up!

The year they were married was the driest in North Dakota's 28 years of statehood. The overall wheat crop was poor, but because of the conflict in Europe, the cash price soared to $3.06 a bushel. In spite of the drouth, there was a spirit of optimism. Even when the federal government established wartime controls in August, 1917, pegging the price of No. 1 Northern at $2.20 in Chicago, the outlook continued to be one of boom and prosperity. Scarcely aware of the inflationary trend about them, the newlyweds returned to Bowen Township where they lived on the Melroe homestead while they began the search for a place of their own. With parental help, they finally made a down-payment on 320 acres just two miles from Oluf's original claim. To get the land, they had to pay $110 an acre, a war-inflated price for property which had been bringing no more than $35 not many months earlier. But they were young, ambitious and hopeful, and Ed had no more doubts about his ability to own his farm than did his father or grandfather before him.

Ed and his bride faced a good life together, one based on love, on the fertile grain-producing soil of North Dakota, on their church and on their kinsmen. Pettersons and Melroes were always nearby, to lend a helping hand or to share a pot of coffee; the two families were well intertwined because Ed's brother, Sig, married Mabel's sister, Myrtle, in 1922, and earlier still, Tillie (Mathilde) Melroe had become Mrs. Ivar Petterson.

On December 6, 1918, Ed and Mabel's first child, Lester Wedell, was born. The 26-year-old father was typically proud of his new son, and somehow the added responsibility seemed to spur him to greater activity in his cluttered

As she stood on the bridal threshold, Mabel Melroe was not convinced that this homestead shack near New England, North Dakota, was an ideal honeymoon cottage.

workshop where he spent much of his time when he wasn't engaged in normal farm chores. Already he was showing his impatience with the quality and performance of the agricultural equipment then on the market.

"Anything he bought at the hardware store or from an implement dealer, he'd have to change," said Mabel. "Sometimes it was just a notch he filed or a bolt he moved, but he was never quite satisfied."

The latter characteristic was to be the dominating theme of Ed Melroe's entire career. It literally drove him to rebuild, to modify, to experiment and to invent. He thoroughly agreed with one of his idols, Thomas Alva Edison, who had proclaimed that the horse was the world's most inefficient engine. Autos and trucks were rapidly replacing Old Dobbin on the nation's streets and highways, and in the fields, an endless variety of tractors was signaling a new era in agriculture. Though he was relatively ill-prepared (two mechanical short courses and his family farm experience), Ed Melroe decided he could build a tractor, too—one which was big enough, fast enough and powerful enough to do the work grain farmers required.

Ed sketched out his ideas and showed them to his father. Oluf recognized an inkling of genius in his son's concepts and agreed to help him build a pilot model. He also liked Ed's plan for a mechanical binder to take some of the handwork out of harvesting unhusked corn. It was agreed that the young inventor should go to a machine shop in Minneapolis and supervise the construction of the two prototypes from the drawings he had made. Mabel bundled up little Lester and accompanied her husband to the Twin Cities, while Ted Melroe "batched" on their farm. For about five months Ed worked closely with the mechanics and machinists at the shop, explaining his blueprints and okaying necessary changes. He was confident that the Lester tractor (to be named for his son) would be a roaring success; then he and his family returned to Bowen Township to await the delivery of the first models. On August 19, 1920, the following story appeared in *The Prairie Press* of Gwinner:

> Mr. E. G. Melroe's new tractor arrived from Minneapolis and is perfect in every detail and one that will find a ready sale when put on the market. It is now being tested on Melroe's farm. A double row corn binder invented by Mr. Melroe also arrived on the same car. It is a labor saver and seems to be the last word in corn binders. Genius Melroe is to be congratulated on his inventions.

It was one of the earliest public notices taken of Ed Melroe's "genius"—and it also introduced him as "E. G.," an initial-name which was to replace "Ed" more and more through the years. Unfortunately, though, his time had not yet come, in spite of the glowing predictions by the Gwinner editor. The tractor never made it to market, though it was used for years on the Melroe farm before it

As a young man, Ed Melroe carefully timed this Heider friction-drive tractor with a stop-watch to learn more about its operation. The machine belonged to neighbor Albert E. Stevens, shown with it.

E. G.'s 1920 corn binder worked, but it had too many "bugs" to be commercially successful.

was dismantled and sold as scrap metal during the Great
Depression. The corn binder worked, too, but it had just
enough "bugs" in it to make it commercially impractical.
E. G. was understandably disappointed, but he was not
discouraged.

The turbulent twenties had begun. Ed continued his
mechanical experimentation, but with a growing family, he
had to concentrate on farm production during the unsteady
economic period following World War I. On December 22,
1920, son Clifford Edward, was born. Then, at two-year
intervals, came Roger Theodore, on October 19, 1922;
Evelyn Mabel, on May 20, 1924; and Irving Lowell, on
February 20, 1926. At the time, neither Ed nor Mabel
could envision the multi-million dollar industry this "family
team" would create just two decades later. After all, Ed's
first attempts at invention had been notably unsuccessful,
and the expense of the failures had proved to be a
considerable financial burden on both himself and his
father for many years after. Nils Petterson, his father-in-
law, also had contributed to the mechanical venture.

In spite of the negative results of E. G.'s first inventive
endeavor, though, Oluf never lost faith in his son's abilities.
Pridefully he would introduce the young man to everyone:
"This is my boy Ed. *He built a tractor!*" The younger
Melroe, meanwhile, had to devote himself to the singular
task of saving the family farm!

The instability of the post-war years was particularly felt
in North Dakota, which, for numerous reasons, had not
progressed far in her efforts to reduce her economic
dependency upon wheat. After the Armistice, the inflationary trend reversed itself. By 1921 wheat was down to
$1.01 a bushel, but even more shattering was the loss in
farm values attributable to deflation. Seventy percent of
the North Dakota farmers were burdened by excessive
mortgages. Many of them, like Ed Melroe, had bought land
for more than $100 an acre and were continuing to pay for
it on that basis, though the property was then worth less

Sig Melroe (left) checked his new bride's batting stance while brother Ted faced an imaginative pitcher. She was Myrtle Petterson, sister of Ed's wife, Mabel.

The 1921 Gwinner Giants included (left to right) Frank Kirk, Oscar Melroe, Carl Peterson, Jack Hurley (later to become a famous fight promoter), Alex Mason, Ted and Sig Melroe.

than half the original price. To make matters worse, North Dakota in the twenties had more banks in proportion to her population than any other state, and many of them had—with great optimism and little collateral—made loans in excess of their total deposits. As a result, 99 of these over-extended financial institutions failed in 1923, and the trend was to continue for an entire decade, affecting two Gwinner banks in the process. Farmers and ranchers failed, too, and the exodus from rural areas began.

During this shaky period, E. G. stayed close to the farm. His crops were generally good, but the substantial obligations created by his farm mortgage and the ill-fated inventions kept him from accumulating any extra cash so he could indulge in his love for mechanical creativity. During the winter months especially, he read the farm publications, noting with fascination the spiraling trend toward mechanization. But there was a frustration involved, too; the demands of his farm and family were such that he could not pursue the many ideas which flashed through his head as he planted, cultivated and harvested his crops from season to season.

He had begun to lease more land in an effort to increase his net return. That meant more equipment, of course, not only to work the additional acreage but to improve the efficiency of his operation. The then-conventional method of harvesting small grain—with the countless man-hours involved in shocking, bundle-pitching and threshing—struck E. G. as an obvious area for improvement. He discussed the matter with his younger brother, Sig, who was farming the original Melroe homestead, and together they decided to do something about it. In 1927 they pooled their resources and bought a new Model P Case combine through Arthur L. Holmstrom, Ed's mechanical compatriot who was to play an important supporting role in the Melroe story.

When the machine finally arrived from the factory by rail, the Melroe brothers hurried to Gwinner to see their

A Case Model P Combine like the one purchased by the Melroes.

acquisition. They found it in a considerable state of dismemberment. With a gallery of local kibitzers on hand to second guess them at every turn of the wrench, Sig and Ed assembled what one local wag called "their over-sized farm toy." The general concensus of the onlookers was that the combine probably wouldn't work in the somewhat rocky ground of Bowen Township. And if it did work, the skeptics concluded, it would never hold up very long!

Chapter 4

A Home-made Pickup and
an Economic Let-down

The purchase of a standard grain combine hardly quali-
fies as an important fact of history—but in the saga of the
Melroe family, the Model P Case was something very
special. It was to be the catalyst which spurred E. G. to
inventive activity and ultimately to generate a family
enterprise which grew beyond the wildest dreams of any of
the participants.

In 1927, though, the Model P was simply another tool to
do a specific farm job, and the Melroe brothers didn't
realize its significance any more than did their neighbors.
The latter were still not sure about the new contraption,

51

The Melroe brothers' new combine was the talk of the township. Leonard Bentson (shown looking down into the machine where Ted Melroe was making repairs) was one of many who came out to the farm to see it work. E. G. was at right in the straw hat.

and they didn't hesitate to express their opinions. Perennial-ly, North Dakota grain was bundled and then stacked in the picturesque shocks which dotted the fields in the late summer. To cut wheat, barley or rye and let it lie on the ground like hay sounded a little foolish.

Ed and Sig, however, knew of the combine's success elsewhere, so they were confident that the machine would prove their detractors wrong. They used the Model P first in the rye fields, and it worked perfectly on "straight combining" of standup grain. The Melroes were elated with their decision to mechanize, but before they moved on to the barley and wheat, the rains came!

For days the brothers were kept out of the fields, and during that period the pesky pigeon grass and other weeds grew up through the grain. When it finally became possible to return to the harvest, the combine simply could not handle the weed-choked, weather-lodged barley. Meanwhile. the other more conservative farmers in the township—with their grain in time-tested shocks for threshing—had no problems, but the Melroe brothers were in plenty of

Marguerite Melroe (Ted's wife) and daughter Helen brought lunch for the header rig crew. Les and Cliff were on the Twin City tractor.

In 1928 E. G. Figured a way to rig up two old McCormick-Deering headers to cut a 24-foot swath of grain. The strung-out gear was somewhat unwieldy but effective.

trouble as much of their year's crop lay matted and unharvestable in the fields. Their pride was hurt, too!

The alternative was to swath the barley into windrows and then use the combine to sweep up the grain as it lay atop the stubble. Hopefully the brothers put the Model P back on the job; this time, though, the pickup attachment—the part of the machine which gathered up the grain-bearing stalks like a giant old-fashioned carpet sweeper—proved woefully inadequate. The dilemma grew worse.

The Melroes heard that the Holt Company in California made a special pickup apparatus for combines, so they drove to Wahpeton and had the dealer there order one by phone. When the gadget finally arrived some ten worrisome days later, it, too, proved relatively useless. The neighbors were apparently right; the combine was an impractical monstrosity, not suited to the conditions in Sargent County. They, of course, didn't consider Ed Melroe's stubborn persistence nor his innate mechanical talents.

At last E. G. had a dire necessity to invent!

There was no simple storybook solution, however. The
frustrated farmers tinkered with the Holt contrivance,
modifying it considerably until it began to retrieve some of
the grain. Brother Ted Melroe, who worked for E. G., was
also involved in the race against the calendar. He recalled
later how the three of them struggled in the fields all day
trying to make the pickup do its proper job; then they'd
stay up half the night repairing and adjusting the apparatus
by gas lantern. There were numerous trips to Art Holmstrom's shop in Gwinner, too, where Ed and his friend
chatted endlessly about the deficiencies of farm machinery
in general and combine pickups in particular. Eventually,
the harvest was completed—at least enough to prevent a
financial disaster—but the Melroes certainly hadn't convinced their neighbors that their newfangled ideas had any
great merit.

They didn't give up, though. The following year the
Model P was back in the field again, this time with a
couple new pickup attachments—neither of which worked
successfully. Ed physically pitched one into a ditch when it
failed to perform, and the brothers went back to the
much-modified Holt. In piecemeal fashion, it was re-built
until it began to function with passable efficiency. Before
the end of the season, Sig and Ed had proved a point, and
in the next two years, three more Case combines arrived at
the Gwinner railroad station; one of them had been ordered
by Nils Petterson, the mutual father-in-law of the Melroe
brothers, who had originally ridiculed the whole idea.

E. G., of course, gave little thought to the potential of
the concept he was developing for a practical combine
pickup; his major concern was for the family harvest.
Besides that, he had a more pressing crisis.

The price of North Dakota farmland had continued to
drop from the unrealistic levels of World War I. Ed and
Mabel Melroe—through no fault of their own—had been the

victims of poor historical timing. For almost a dozen years they had held on, trying to protect a $10,000 down-payment and their ensuing investment. Unfortunately, in 1929 their $110-an-acre land had slipped to less than a third of that value, and the disparity simply caught up with them. For the Melroes, the Crash of '29 came early; their mortgage was foreclosed, and they lost their farm!

The Melroe youngsters and their dog, "Jiggs." Left to right, back row: Roger, Clifford and Les; front row: Evelyn and Irving.

Once again Ed Melroe demonstrated his Norwegian tenacity and pride. He couldn't quit; he had five growing children to feed, a share of a 1927 combine to pay for and a personal anathema for failure. He and Mabel got into their Flint auto, drove eastward a half mile up the road and obligated themselves for another farm — this time for $35 an acre.

At the time, the Melroe youngsters had little knowledge of their parents' financial difficulties. There was some question about why they had to leave a nice, comfortable farm home for a less adequate dwelling, but youngsters have a way of adapting, and Grandpa Oluf showed up with his carpenter tools to help E. G. make the necessary improvements. The move itself was a short one, and the older boys didn't even have to change schools. Their father built an enclosed two-wheeled cart to protect them from the weather, and their old horse "Florida" clip-clopped

This bank building has been the scene of financial stress and strain, target of the "Great Gwinner bank robbery" and later the home of the local restaurant.

down the road to Bowen No. 3 as before. Life continued pretty much as usual, and though the stock market on far-away Wall Street had plummeted, the real Big News in Gwinner, North Dakota, had been the robbery of a local bank by four big-city hoodlums in August. They had been spotted in the attempt, and five young men from the community—Ruben, Elmer and Leonard Bentson; Carl and Ben Meinhardt—whipped the gangsters in a gun battle and foiled their get-away. Later a posse of almost 300 area citizens rounded up the quartet of frustrated and buck-shot-peppered bandits who didn't realize that Gwinner was an unusual town.

Gradually the community settled back to normalcy until two years later, on October 22, 1931, *The Prairie Press* carried the following headline:

GWINNER BANK CLOSED
Great Shock to the Community

The economic depression, already being felt intensely in other parts of the nation, had finally come to Sargent County!

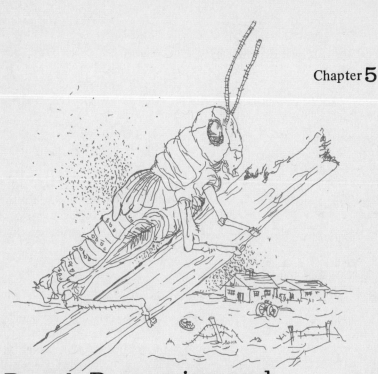

Chapter 5

Drouth, Depression and a Double-duty Dam

At first the economic calamity which befell the country did not materially affect life on the Melroe farm. *The Prairie Press* of January 29, 1931, reported:

> Mr. and Mrs. Ed Melroe went to Oakes with some turkeys last Thursday and also took in the talking picture in the evening.

On February 12 the paper announced:

> Mr. and Mrs. Carl Swanson and family were visitors at the Ed Melroe home Saturday night. Mrs. Ed Melroe was sure hard on her new piano, while Ted Flynn and Einar Swanson were doing the singing.

A month later the editor wrote that the Sargent County courthouse in Forman was "packed with citizens" trying to get tax relief. The same issue noted that No. 1 durum had dipped to 47 cents a bushel. Beginning in 1929, hot winds and reduced rainfall had aggravated the situation, especially in northwestern North Dakota and eastern Montana. By autumn an appeal was made to the farmers of Sargent County (who had not been as hard hit) to help the destitute people in the disaster areas. Children were dressed in made-over feed sacks; Russian thistles were pickled for what little food value could be obtained from them; there were even a few cases of hungry families trying to exist on salted-down gophers, according to the news stories of the day.

In Bowen Township Ed Melroe had a further reason for perfecting an efficient combine pickup. Every kernel of

Following the lead of his brothers-in-law (Ed and Sig Melroe), Ivar Petterson—with his son, Karyl—built an extra-wide swather from two smaller headers.

grain was needed to feed the impoverished, but lack of moisture had resulted in "short straw" which was difficult to harvest. E. G. searched through junk piles at home, in Gwinner and Oakes, looking for parts to build a practical mechanism which would "sweep" *all* the cut grain from the field, not just some of it. An old muck elevator used by a

road contractor provided belting for the pickup apron;
rollers came from a worn-out pushbinder; a cut-down auto
chassis supplied the frame. From such odds-and-ends, E. G.
put together a pilot model for himself and Sig. He made
similar attachments for Albert Stevens, Nils Petterson and
Alvin Orth. They were anything but standard, of course,
because when he ran out of one type of material, he went
to the scrap heap and adapted something else. He didn't
consider himself in the manufacturing business; he was
merely trying to help himself, his brothers and his neighbors harvest a very slim grain crop. But know it or not, he
had started a chain of unplanned events which—in the years
ahead—was to create a unique family enterprise.

For the time being, though, there were other things to
think about. The Gwinner bank failure had shaken the
confidence of some of the local farmers. Maintaining one's
morale was not easy when wheat dropped to 36 cents and
oats to nine. To get a little capital, Ed shipped a load of
hogs to Fargo—but the driver came back with a bill for
$5.40. The hogs hadn't brought enough to cover the cost
of their transportation to market.

Still, fortunately, there were no bread lines in Gwinner
as there were elsewhere in the land. To keep their children
fed, E. G. and Mabel milked cows, raised chickens and
planted a big garden. For the family larder, he butchered
the animals which had almost no value in the marketplace.
He also gave haircuts, repaired worn-out shoes and did
whatever else he could to achieve a measure of self-suffi-
ciency on the farm. Mabel shuddered when he used her
foot-pedalled Sears sewing machine to patch up deteriorat-
ing canvas on his old equipment.

Most of the children were not aware of the national
panic. The boys had been playing baseball "from the time
they could first walk"—and a depression didn't take that
away. During the winter, they had fun on the toboggan
their father had built out of scrap lumber and the iron tires

taken from old buggy wheels. It was especially exciting to
try to stand up when "Birdie," the family horse, pulled
them across the snow. Roger tried it once too often, fell
and broke his leg. E. G. loaded him into the box of the
Flint truck and hauled him to Forman to have the bone
set. The "truck," incidentally, was really the old family
auto rebuilt; on Sundays the Melroes rode to church service
in Gwinner in it, mother and father up front, the youngsters in the rear.

Ed also built another enclosed school wagon for the
children, a four-wheeler this time because there were more
passengers. He showed continuing interest in their educa-
tion, particularly stressing penmanship which he considered
both disciplinary and a mark of personal achievement.

"He believed in the Palmer Method and had us do page after page
of ovals and push-pulls," said
daughter Evelyn, recalling long
sessions around the oilcloth-
covered kitchen table under
the Aladdin Lamp ("the best
light in the house").

The same table was the setting for literally thousands of
games of whist.

In 1933 conditions got worse instead of better. The
rainfall average for North Dakota—13.5 inches—was the
fourth lowest in the state's history. Added to that, a
massive hatch of grasshoppers raised havoc with what
scanty crops the farmers were able to grow. With their
perpetual motion mandibles, the 'hoppers cut binder twine,
nibbled at clothing on wash lines, gnawed at pitchfork
handles and literally devoured entire fields of grain.

Only 9.5 inches of precipitation fell in 1934, the driest
year to that time. Grasshopper control crews worked
feverishly—sometimes on barren, sun-scorched earth—to
spread their poison bait of molasses, bran, arsenic and
water. (Skeptics claimed that the only insects they killed
were the ones they ran over putting the bait out.) Dust
clouds blew across the state, drifting along fence rows and

against farm buildings deserted by beaten, despairing families. With the sun unable to penetrate the eerie, sepia-toned
haze, kerosene lamps burned at mid-day in the Melroe
kitchen. In spite of the bleak prospects for the future, E.
G. managed to impress upon his youngsters that their home
was more important than luxuries—and that as long as they
had the mutual strength and love of one another, they
would never really be poor.

Economically, though, North Dakota was truly poor,
hurt more by the depression and the accompanying natural
catastrophes than almost any other state. From 1932
through 1937 the per capita personal income in North
Dakota was only 47 percent of the national average. In the
same period, the unpaid general property taxes amounted
to more than $34 million. Thousands of families lost their
farms through foreclosures and forced sales. Many of them
fled the stricken state—a great majority to Washington,

Oregon and California. Federal money was poured into North Dakota, some $266 million from 1933 through 1940. By 1935, 37 percent of the population was receiving some form of relief—and the end was not in sight.

The Civil Works Administration was followed by the Federal Emergency Relief Administration, which in turn was succeeded by the Works Progress Administration. Ed Melroe, then in his mid-forties, struggled to hold on. A normal rainfall in 1935 had helped somewhat, but wheat rust, an untimely hail storm and continuing low prices negated any strong comeback. Mabel's chicken flock—between 400 and 500 layers—just barely paid the grocery bills and the dollar-a-week (plus room-and-board) for the hired man. The boys gathered and sold scrap metal, which their father prophetically warned "would some day come back at us."

Personal sorrow also visited them that summer, as Oluf Melroe—the determined, sometimes short-tempered, often jovial Norwegian immigrant—died on June 26 at the age of 86. Included among the pallbearers were his sons Ed, Oscar, Sig and Ted. Mabel's mother, Selma Petterson, passed away less than a month later, on July 22. (Nils Petterson did not live to see the end of the depression either; he died on October 20, 1937.)

In 1936, the drouth struck again with full fury. The state recorded the lowest and highest temperatures ever experienced within a five-month period—60 degrees below zero at Parshall on February 15 and 121 degrees above at Steele on July 6. The average annual rainfall plummeted to a nadir of 8.8 inches. It was probably the most difficult year of E. G. Melroe's life, as he swallowed his pride and took a supervisory job on a W.P.A. project. Not that he minded the work; he'd been accustomed to rough menial labor since he was a boy. He was, however, a conservative, independent-minded believer in individual enterprise, and when he found himself forced to partake of the largesse of the federal government, the emotional pill was almost too enormous to swallow. Moreover, he wasn't sold on the dam project which government engineers had assigned to him and his crew in the slightly rolling land southwest of Gwinner. In later years, a local jester described the dam as twice as good as any other; it held back water on both sides!

As was the case with many men of his generation, E. G. became embittered at the policies of President Franklin D. Roosevelt's administration which, he felt, caused good people to become shiftless and shiftless ones to prosper as happy supplicants at the federal trough. Though his oldest boy, Les, spent six months in the Civilian Conservation Corps, Ed even refused to credit F. D. R. with such obvious agricultural improvements as depression-planted shelterbelts and reforestation projects.

"It was Theodore Roosevelt's idea," he always said, and that ended the conversation.

Under the circumstances, he vowed he would make it on his own, whether it meant working twice as hard on the land—or possibly manufacturing a few combine pickups for sale to the farmers who had begun to inquire about them. Maybe his wooden haystack form and elevator, invented in 1936, would be marketable. (It wasn't!) After all, things *had* to get better; they couldn't get much worse!

In the midst of the depression, E. G. invented this haystack form and belt-driven elevator. It was too unwieldy, so he junked it after a year.

The boys, meanwhile, gathered and washed eggs—which they hated to do. They also milked a small herd of cows every morning and night—which they hated even more. They got into milk fights, of course, and after they had grown up, they admitted that they had added water to the buckets a few times so their father couldn't tell how much they had spilled. On dance nights, they'd "accidentally" turn the calves loose to do the milking for them.

They also had a family ice enterprise, cutting blocks in the impoundment behind the W.P.A. dam or freezing water in an old pit silo at home. On Friday nights they got free tickets for providing enough ice to keep the beer and soda pop cold in the stock tank at Red Smith's weekly barn dance. They also had an "Ice For Sale" sign on the road in front of the farm, but when relatives came, Mabel would send one of the boys down to chip a bushel basket full for which there was never any charge. This didn't make good business sense to the youngsters who promptly took paint

and brush and painted on the back side of the road sign:
"Not Free to Relatives."

Needless to say, they got a good Scandinavian dressing
down when their mother found out about it!

In 1937 a glimmer of better things ahead brought
encouragement to the long-suffering North Dakota farmers.
For more than half a decade, the emphasis had been on
simple survival; as tenacious as he was, even Ed Melroe was
ready for a brighter horizon.

Chapter 6

A Wooden Leg
and a Will of Iron

In the spring of 1937 a ripple of optimism began to make itself felt in the down-but-never-out state of North Dakota. At the Melroe farm in Sargent County, this feeling that the worst was past pervaded the entire family as the croplands were prepared for another growing season.

It was obvious that Ed Melroe had no intentions of leaving the soil as so many others had done. Consequently, representatives of insurance companies and other property agents virtually stood in line to offer him land for lease or for sale. Untilled and unproductive, the numerous foreclosed farms were merely a tax burden for those who had acquired them. The situation presented an unusual oppor-

69

tunity for anyone who was willing to take a chance, and E.
G. asked himself: "What can I lose?" He had been down to
rock-bottom before, and somehow his family survived without too much suffering. And so he plunged!

In 1936 he had expanded from three quarter sections
(160 acres each) to seven; a year later he more than
doubled that total. Much of the land was leased, of course,
but he picked up several quarters at tax title auctions for
$5 to $15 an acre. By 1938 he was farming some 3,500
acres.

This necessitated an increased equipment inventory, so
Ed was a familiar figure at the disposal sales then so
prevalent throughout the beleagured area. For $100 or less
he bought weary old tractors and other well-worn machines. These he hauled home to be restored and occasionally modified by himself and sons, Lester and Cliff.

When Ed Melroe expanded his farm operation after 1937, he bought used,
broken-down equipment wherever he could. With his sons and brother Ted, he
then restored the machinery to working condition. Here E. G. inspected a
Model P Case combine (purchased from Alvin Orth) and a Model LA Case
tractor.

"They were junk when we got them," Les remembered,
"but once they were overhauled, they gave us reasonably
good service. After that, we were continually upgrading."

This willingness to start at the bottom and work up was to be a keynote of E. G.'s ultimate success. Still, the climb upward was not easy. Field work was seemingly endless. Then, in the evenings—or when rains came to make it impossible to venture out onto the land—the family made combine pickups, two or three in 1937 and more than a dozen in 1938. All the work was by hand; there was no electricity on the farm for power tools even if Ed could have afforded them. Model T and Model A Ford frames were hacksawed apart and used to form the basic unit. Wire for the pickup teeth came in coils and was cut to the proper length on an anvil with a cold chisel. Old lawn mower wheels provided the running gear. The extra money which came from these somewhat crude combine attachments was a great boon to the Melroe comeback endeavor.

Because of the extent of his farming operation and his pre-occupation with the pickup invention, E. G. kept at least two hired men on the place. They worked for $35 a month and "Mabel's cooking." The latter was a bonus factor which aided immeasurably in retaining good help on the limited payroll. In her recollections of the period, Mabel looked back with no regrets to the passing of a brief fad in male attire during the late thirties. Almost as if it were a sartorial symbol of brighter days ahead, the men were caught up in a fleeting style which was hardly practical in a farm community like Bowen Township. For dress-up, they all wore white shirts and white trousers—and every Monday morning, Mabel and her gas-engine Maytag washer faced the unenviable task of refurbishing at least seven sets of "whites" for the following weekend. Daughter Evelyn helped with the mountainous ironing.

On Sunday afternoon, June 18, 1939, Ed, Mabel and Evelyn drove to Grand Rapids Park near LaMoure to attend a church picnic. (In Melroe tradition, the boys were playing baseball elsewhere.) Reverend E. E. Bostrom had scheduled the event so that his congregation could relax after a rigorous period of remodeling the old Gustaf Adolf Lutheran Church which had been built in 1899 and moved to

The Gustaf Adolf Lutheran Church was towed into Gwinner by two steam tractors in 1908.

Gwinner with the help of two steam tractors in the winter of 1907-08. The day was pleasant, and as usual there was a bat and ball available for the traditional softball game. E. G., despite his 47 years, couldn't wait to get on the diamond to show the young folks how the Melroe brothers used to do it in the good old days.

Fatefully and tragically, the sport he loved so well was to deliver a cruel blow to a seemingly robust and healthy farmer. (He was 5 feet 11 inches tall and weighed approximately 230 pounds at the time.) Ed's heart rebelled, and he fell in a crumpled, pain-stricken heap on the ball field. He was taken to the Peter Albertson home in LaMoure where for more than a week his condition remained critical. Then, when he had shown sufficient improvement, he was moved to the hospital in Oakes. The battle against the heart attack was apparently being won, but complications arose with the lodging of a blood clot in his left leg. Dr. F. E. Wolfe, the attending physician, called in specialists for consultation, and when no other course of action seemed advisable, the decision was made to amputate above the knee. Doctor Wolfe didn't perform the operation himself, but he insisted upon serving as anesthesiologist so that he could keep a close eye on his patient and friend. (The doctor, whom the Melroe family credited with saving E. G.'s life, ironically was to lose both his legs by amputation in later years.)

This new physical impairment was not easy for Ed Melroe to accept. Being strong-willed, he could stand the pain and discomfiture; but the loss of mobility, just at a time when life was on the upswing for him and his family, caused him considerable mental anguish. With some 20 quarters under tillage, he felt he was needed in the field, even though his brother Ted had returned to North Dakota to help out following E. G.'s heart attack. Furthermore, Ed's combine pickup had begun to attract attention beyond Sargent County and he had intended to step up production. In addition, the expenses of his illness and surgery weighed heavily upon him.

Among the keen observers of the Melroe pickup was the John Deere Company. The attachment, the corporation's engineers concluded, would be a valuable addition to their machines as standard equipment. E. G. received an offer for the rights to his invention, and under the circumstances—he decided to sell Patent No. 2,253,797 which had been granted to him on August 26, 1941. In time, the mail brought a check for $5,000 and immediately some of his financial pressures were removed.

E. G., meanwhile, wasn't satisfied with his wooden leg

E. G. MELROE

GRAIN PICKUP FOR COMBINES

Filed Dec. 9, 1940   4 Sheets—Sheet 3

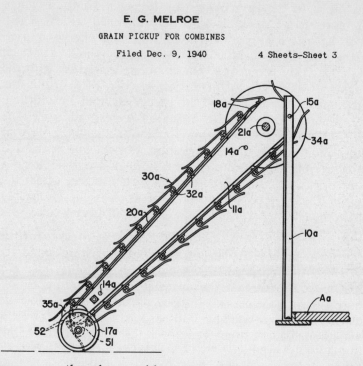

any more than he would accept a piece of farm equipment
without at least some slight modification. The first one he
got in Fargo was too heavy and caused him considerable
pain, so he whittled on it and readjusted it continually in
search of improvement. Finally he made an artificial limb
of his own design out of light-weight wooden slats. Though
it did not have knee-action, he preferred it to the commercial models. His involvement with the mechanics of his
walking aid helped take his mind off the disability itself.

During the trying period of adjustment, he revised his
plans for the future. After all, he was really getting too old
to play the outfield, and his boys were big enough to
assume greater responsibility for the farm work. Oh, they
horsed around a little bit—like the time or two Irv went
galavanting across a field with tractor and combine in
pursuit of a mouse . . . or when Les tried physically to

(Left) Like any other brothers, the Melroes scuffled occasionally, and in 1938 Cliff came out second-best in a physical encounter with Les. The reason? Les was trying to convince his younger brother that the latter should go to college. (Right) James Dahl and Irv Melroe in costume for a Gwinner high school play.

convince Cliff that the latter should go to college, and in the tussle on the back of an old truck Cliff fell and ended up with his arm in a grotesque brace. Generally, though, they got their chores done satisfactorily before they hustled off to the baseball diamond so that E. G. didn't have to worry too much about the farm falling apart at the seams. Maybe—he thought—in spite of his limitations, he could devote a little more time to a few ideas he had to improve further the harvesting of grain.

Chapter 7

World War II: The Great Interim

December 7, 1941, brought a new anxiety to Ed and Mabel Melroe. With four sons at or near military age, they could not help but view the Japanese attack on Pearl Harbor from a position of personal concern.

When the infamous raid occurred, Roger was already in uniform. He had played trombone in high school, and during his senior year, he and several of his friends enlisted in the 164th Infantry Regiment band, a National Guard unit headquartered in Lisbon. The dollar-a-meeting had considerable influence on the teen-age musicians who soon found themselves on active duty at Camp Claiborne, Louisiana. On Pearl Harbor day the regiment was dispatched to Washington State to guard strategic sites; early in 1942 it was sent to Australia, and ultimately Roger landed in Guadalcanal with a rifle instead of a trombone.

77

The Melroes were reunited for this war-time photo in the mid-1940's. Left to right, back row: Roger, Les, Evelyn, Irving and Clifford; front row: Mabel and E. G.

Les, too, signed on with the army, serving with engineering construction groups in Europe; when he was old enough, Irv joined the Navy. Clifford, who in mechanical interest and native ability was most like his father, applied for enlistment in the Army Air Corps. However, a physician's stethoscope ruled out his acceptance, and the disappointed young man came home in a state of dejection. As it turned out, he was "in service," too. The Melroe

Oct. 2, 1951   E. G. MELROE   2,570,065
                 PICKUP DEVICE FOR HARVESTERS
Filed May 18, 1949   2 Sheets-Sheet 2

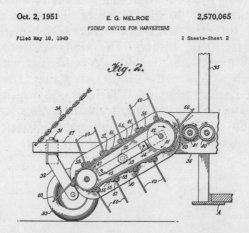

farm—like others across the nation—was vital to the war effort, and Cliff's presence at home was desperately needed.

Meanwhile, E. G. had a new burst of inventive enthusiasm. The pickup patent purchased by John Deere was a

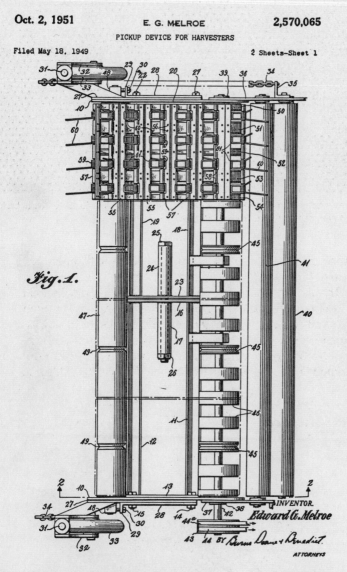

Oct. 2, 1951   E. G. MELROE   2,570,065
PICKUP DEVICE FOR HARVESTERS
Filed May 18, 1949   2 Sheets—Sheet 1

These are the basic patent drawings for E. G.'s new-style pickup.

belt-type conveyor of canvas on which spring-steel teeth
were rigidly fastened. It was an effective apparatus, but Ed
had already begun to experiment on a new design in which
the teeth were hinged so that they would be extended to
sweep up the straw and carry it to the combine's canvas
platform or auger. Then they would drop flat to release
their load before traveling again to the "pickup" position.
In practice the device proved even more efficient than the
original patent, and Ed was faced with several decisions.

E. G. Melroe was a good farmer and an imaginative one. He was not afraid to
try new crops and new techniques—but he was a vocal and practicing exponent
of soil conservation and replenishment. "You can't get something out of the
land if you don't put something back into it," he always said.

First of all, he and his family moved into Gwinner. Then he acquired an abandoned service station which he fitted up as a shop. If he were to produce combine pickups in any quantity, he needed electric power. Hand drills, cold chisels and hacksaws were all right for a few products, but volume required mechanization. Actually, he was not yet ready to establish a manufacturing business; the war precluded that. He also had to oversee his farm operation which, of necessity, had to be somewhat curtailed. To prove that he was still willing to try something new, however, he planted a crop of mustard.

"It's a weed, so it ought to grow well in North Dakota," he facetiously announced.

Lunch-time on one of the Melroe quarters in 1943. (Left to right, seated): Robert Bentson, Clarence Hegle, Irv and Cliff Melroe; (standing) Harold Jacobson.

During the war, limited numbers of the new-style pickups were built in the old gas station. They were eagerly snapped up by local farmers, anxious to find mechanical help of any kind in the labor-scarce years. For the Melroes—like so many other American families—World War II was the Great Interim, a period of marking time until sons, husbands and fathers returned. Ed and Mabel were fortunate; their three boys escaped the war unscratched. At home, though E. G. further complicated his means of locomotion. He had been crossing a street in Fargo with his friend and confidante, Art Holmstrom, when he slipped on the ice and fell. The wooden leg broke and ended up somewhere behind Ed's neck. Not realizing that an artificial limb was involved, a passerby gasped in horror at the grotesque contortions of the big man on the pavement. The situation had a touch of macabre humor, but Ed had also fractured his right ankle which was anything but a laughing matter. When he finally got home to Gwinner, he fashioned a walker out of a steel kitchen chair with casters so that he could at least get around the house.

Art Holmstrom continued to be an important factor in E. G.'s personal saga. Not only did the Gwinner Case dealer sell the Melroe brothers the Model P combine which generated the first pickup, but he was always available as a valued adviser and sounding board for Ed's latest ideas. Art himself had an inventive mind and had acquired a patent on an ingenious automobile gas guage. Time after time, Ed would stop at Art's shop with his family in the car. "I'll be back in just a minute," he'd tell Mabel. An hour or more later he and his fellow inventor would still be deep in mechanical conversation. His wife and his children learned to accept these lengthy discussions as a part of their normal pattern of existence. In addition, Mabel had to undergo similar waiting sessions in the family auto whenever she accompanied Ed to the Fargo Foundry for special castings and other needs of his experimentation. When his mind was on mechanics, he lost all track of time!

If there was a bright side at all to E. G.'s physical handicap, though, it was that it forced him to become a better manager. He could no longer do everything himself, so he learned to delegate work and responsibilities. The experience was also valuable to Cliff, who in a few short years was to assume an unexpectedly important executive role.

Crops and prices were generally good during the war, and in spite of the necessary restrictions, E. G. was able to recoup some of the losses of the thirties. At the same time, he and Mabel were able to take winter trips to California, Texas and Florida, not only to find relief from the continual pain in his leg but to satisfy somewhat a life-long interest in other parts of the nation and the world.

"Dad was an avid reader of the *National Geographic*," daughter Evelyn said. "Through it he learned about every continent on the globe. His knowledge of foreign lands was quite fantastic."

Following his physical impairment, E. G. and Mabel began to travel more, especially during the winter months when the North Dakota cold added to his discomfiture. Ed was pictured here with neighbor Everett Stevens, who with his wife, Frances, accompanied the Melroes to Texas in 1943.

Mabel and E. G. during a trip to California in the mid 1940's.

While he worked and traveled, E. G. contemplated the economic storms he had weathered, and more and more he began to think about some form of family enterprise which would keep all his youngsters together once Les, Rog and Irv completed their service obligations. Ole J. Dahl, the village storekeeper and one of Ed's whist-playing cronies, had dreamt that the Melroes would some day have a big factory in Gwinner on the site of the old tourist park. As it turned out, he was prophetic even to the location!

Chapter 8

Gwinner, of All Places!

Unlike many other former servicemen whose military travels lured them to new localities, the Melroe brothers all came home to Gwinner when the war was over. There were no grand visions of industrial success; they merely wanted to get back to a way of life which they had learned to appreciate even more so during their involuntary meanderings.

Roger returned to school briefly at the University of North Dakota, while Irv and Les joined Cliff in the re-expanded farm operation. They dug out their old baseball gloves and formed a new edition of the Gwinner

Giants. They could, at one time, field an all-kinsmen team, with Irv at first base, Rog at second, Les, Cliff and Uncle Ted in the outfield; Sig's boys Sylvan and Stan at shortstop and third base, respectively; and cousin-by-marriage, Ruben (Rub) Bentson, catching, and cousin Edgar (Bud) Petterson, pitching. In American Legion baseball, the latter once pitched a better-than-perfect seven-inning game, striking out all 22 of the batters who faced him; the catcher dropped the ball on one strikeout and the runner was safe at first. Uncle Sig managed the team, incidentally, and every now and then took a turn as a pinch-hitter.

Meanwhile, there were a few local orders for combine pickups, and the boys helped E. G. assemble them. Informally, they discussed the potential of the harvesting device and decided they should make the most of it, especially since the farm operation offered a source of capital and a hedge against possible failure. They never did officially establish a business; it just sort of *happened,* and Gwinner, North Dakota, found itself with a manufacturing company, though the latter was still housed in a vacated service station and offered little evidence of future greatness.

Gwinner itself didn't have much going for it. Counting two or three stray dogs, the salesmen who called on O. J. Dahl's grocery store and the daily bread-truck driver, the dwindling hamlet had a population of almost 200 in 1947. Less than a half century old, it was the type of town which theoretical sociologists were already dooming to extinction.

In 1900 the Northern Pacific had established it as a railroad station when the line was pushed westward from Milnor to Oakes. The company was having trouble labeling all the tiny new settlements it was creating along its various rights-of-way, and when the station in White Stone Hill Township was built, railroad officials reached all the way to Germany for a name. Artur von Gwinner, a director of the influential Deutsche Bank of Berlin (which was heavily invested in the Northern Pacific), was duly honored. He was a director of the Anatolian and Baghdad railways in Turkey, a noted financier and political expert, a collector of botanical and mineral specimens and a member of the German House of Lords. In spite of the credentials, his name was not a particularly appropriate choice since the area was almost entirely populated by Norwegians and Swedes; the German-Russians, of whom North Dakota had attracted thousands, homesteaded to the north and west.

Gwinner was actually preceded in White Stone Hill Township by a postoffice known as Forsby. On May 15, 1901, Josephine A. Carlblom, wife of the village storekeeper, was named Gwinner's first postmistress. That same year the townsite was surveyed and platted. A hotel was built in 1902, and a year later H. W. Spencer printed Volume 1, Number 1 of his weekly *Prairie Press*. In 1904 the State Bank of Gwinner opened its doors with a total capital of $15,000. Nels Bjork was the first harness-maker; Fred Rehborg started a lumberyard and hardware store; Alton Olson was the village blacksmith; and H. O. Barlow was the first school teacher. Of the latter, Nils Petterson, in a brief

Main Street of Gwinner, looking northward, had hardly changed in four decades following World War I—except for the addition of more automobiles and the Melroe brothers: Les, Cliff, Rog and Irv.

Gwinner's Main Street (looking south) was not particularly impressive following World War I, nor did it change much in the next quarter-century. The brick building at left housed the bank which was robbed in 1929, and at one time Ted Melroe operated a restaurant in it.

history of the township, wrote "He had no training whatever . . . he could raise horseradish and rutabagas better."

White Stone Hill Township had been surveyed in 1882, a year after the Ole F. Johnson and Fred Carlblom families arrived by oxen and covered wagon from Minnesota. Its name supposedly originated in a case of mistaken identity—the erroneous belief that the Battle of Whitestone Hill on September 3, 1863 (North Dakota's bloodiest Indian fray), was fought on the site and not in the vicinity of Merricourt in Dickey County. The slight promontory north of Gwinner was known by the Indians as "Dead Colt Hill," so named because—in ages past—a grieving brave, whose pinto pony had died in a raging snowstorm, reputedly buried the animal on top of the ridge. Other Indians, who also lost horses in the blizzard, were said to have done the same.

I. N. Nicolett visited the area in 1839 with John C. Fremont, and a map he drew designated the site according to the Indian tradition. In the hills was a crystal pure spring near which the Indians camped on their nomadic trail between the prairies and the Turtle Mountains on the Canadian border. Later the so-called Government Road, used by settlers and Indians traveling southward from Fort Ransom, passed the cool water spring. Before the first artesian well was dug in the township in 1902, homesteaders hauled household water from the natural fountain. According to Nils Petterson, "sometimes as many as 20 ox teams were lined up," with the pioneers waiting to dip water into tanks, barrels, buckets and other containers.

Such was the relatively inauspicious beginning of Gwinner and the surrounding township. In its first 47 years, it gave little promise of being anything more than a sleepy rail town where farmers could come to deliver their grain and do their basic shopping. The Northern Pacific's line from Wahpeton to Oakes—despite such illustrious German names as von Gwinner and Count Friedrich zu Limburg Stirum on the stations between—never became more than a secondary freight route, and highway access was poorer still. In time, state highways 13 and 32 junctioned just east of the village, but through-traffic was rare, and Gwinner profited little from what there was.

By every criterion, the Sargent County hamlet was a most illogical place to start a manufacturing company. It was "too far from anywhere." Everything had to be shipped in and shipped out. There simply weren't enough people to provide a labor pool. When the Melroe family decided to go into the pickup-building business in an expanded way, it was just a replay of the old story about the bumblebee which scientists said had too much weight for its wing-span, and therefore, shouldn't be able to fly—but the bumblebee didn't know this, so it flew anyhow. Totally unsophisticated in the world of industry, E. G. Melroe and sons didn't know that Gwinner was an impossible place to do business, and as a result, when they "flew anyhow," the tiny town and the entire state of North Dakota were the better for it!

The Melroe factory now stands on the site of Gwinner's disastrous town fire of 1921. (Top) Before; (below) after. Ted and E. G. Melroe helped save the elevator in the background (lower picture) by hosing it down as the flames crept toward it.

Chapter 9

A Dream Takes Shape

As years pass, the stories of nations, individuals and business firms tend to be reduced to highlights. In the process, the day-by-day anxieties, crises and failures are often lost in the historical shuffle. In a rags-to-riches saga like that of the Melroes, a few noteworthy dates, several key events and a rocketing sales graph seem to indicate a no-strain, no-pain ride to instant success.

But that wasn't the way it happened!

E. G. Melroe didn't just invent a gadget, dream a dream and then create—with no problems or pitfalls—a full-blown industry. As a matter of fact, even after the decision to move ahead was made, he was reluctant to plunge quite as aggressively as his enthusiastic sons wanted to do. It took their exuberance to offset his conservatism, born of a disastrous inflation-deflation experience, his personal recollections of the economic depression and a firsthand understanding of the fickleness of North Dakota weather.

In the formative year of 1946, the plant was moved to an old schoolhouse, which was certainly not much of an improvement. In the fall of 1947 an opportunity arose to buy a used punch press, drill press and turning lathe, all for $1,000. E. G. was reticent, but the boys prevailed. When the equipment arrived from Minneapolis, the family was committed to manufacturing. Before that there was little capital investment other than in tools common to most farm operations and a homemade punch press fashioned from the gears of a McCormick-Deering hay mower and a one-cylinder Fairbanks-Morse gas engine. Ed Melroe recognized the dividing line, but to his credit, he gave his sons loose rein, and the future of the entire family was changed.

That included daughter Evelyn and her new husband, Eugene R. Dahl, son of the Gwinner grocer who had foretold the Melroe factory. They were married on December 21, 1947, and Gene was to join the firm in 1950 to complete the original family management lineup.

Then there was the matter of sales. Up to that time nobody really *sold* a Melroe pickup; the neighbors liked what E. G. was producing on a part-time basis, so they came by and bought one. That's what happened in the case of William G. Bruns, a glib North Dakota farmer from the western Sargent County community of Crete. Bruns liked what he bought, and without the formality of hiring, he simply "went to work" for the Melroe firm. He was so effective in his visits with the farmers in the area that he sold more than 100 attachments in just one season; what's more, he collected $50 in advance from some of the purchasers to give E. G. and his sons the working capital to buy the necessary materials and parts.

Bill Bruns helped get the Melroe Manufacturing Company off the ground. He sold pickups on a loose, informal commission arrangement, mostly because no other system had yet been considered. He liked it that way. "They can't fire me," he said with a smile, "because I've never been on the payroll."

The first two years brought a melange of major and minor problems. There were 22 quarters of land to farm, for without the revenue, the company would have been in financial straits from the moment it opened its doors. Through a misunderstanding, someone in the John Deere Company threatened a patent suit, and Roger was dispatched to head off the litigation. Though he was still in his mid-twenties and had no experience in business law, he managed (with legal counsel) to achieve a complete release for the production of the new-style pickup. Later, E. G. and Ted Melroe drove to Washington, D. C., with their wives, and there the two men finally resolved the patent squabble by successfully presenting the points of difference between the two pickup concepts.

Meanwhile, largely because of Bill Bruns' sales success and the acquisition of the second-hand equipment, it was apparent that the schoolhouse was no place for a manufacturing company on the move. Consequently, the construction of a new building was proposed.

Again E. G. was skeptical, and again his sons had to do some fast talking to convince him that they needed elbow room to produce combine attachments in the quantities they had optimistically envisioned. Ed finally agreed, and a 30x100 cement block building—all a single large room except for a cracker-box office in one corner—was built a block east of Gwinner's Main Street. When the rather

The Melroe Windrow Pickup evolved from the homemade model (top) into a standardized commercial version soon after World War II (bottom). The earliest attachments featured cast-off parts and spring teeth cut and twisted by hand.

unimpressive sign, announcing the "Melroe Mfg. Co." went up over the front door, the five partners were as proud as if they'd erected an industrial Taj Mahal on the North Dakota prairie. From that point on, there was no turning back!

The company plan was very simple: Les, Irv and Rog were to sell pickups in the late fall and winter; E. G. and Cliff were to work on the development of the product and to prepare for a production schedule; in the winter and whenever field work didn't interfere, everybody—including the hired men—would go on the assembly line. Anyway that's how it was supposed to work, but with the pressures of farm chores, the summer baseball schedule (the Gwinner Giants still needed the Melroes) and the family's natural tendency for unregimented action, the business got started pretty much on a catch-as-catch-can basis.

The selling phase was especially a learn-as-you-go process. "It was like Major Bowes' Amateur Hour," one of the boys recalled.

Irv, for instance, was assigned the state of South Dakota

as his territory. Still in his early twenties, he scheduled his first dealer call on the H. C. Clark Implement Company of Aberdeen. He was, as he put it, like a country bumpkin going to town with a basket of eggs to sell—except that you didn't have to explain an egg to every buyer. For half a day he drove around the town, trying to get up nerve enough to see Harland Clark. Finally, he steeled himself for the inevitable and went in, not so much because of a great urge to sell because he knew his brothers would razz the devil out of him if he failed on his first mission. He had no business cards, no expense account and no fancy literature; but he did know the product, and Clark showed him the courtesy of listening to his baptismal pitch. The price of a Melroe pickup was almost twice that of any others on the market, but Clark liked the idea of the "floating action" which permitted E. G.'s device to follow the contour of the field independently of the combine itself. He promptly

E. G. was somewhat skeptical when his sons proposed to erect the company's first factory building. It was completed in 1948.

ordered a couple, on *consignment.*

Irv, unfortunately, had never heard of the word, but with his naturally easy manner, the embryonic salesman

worked his way out of the embarrassment and ultimately
signed Clark as one of the Melroe's earliest dealers. Later
Irv learned that brother Les had run into the same word
problem when he called on his first customers—John
Oksness of Doran, Minnesota, and Ben Kilde of Fergus
Falls. Les didn't know what consignment meant either!

In spite of the stuttering start, the new firm began to
flourish—at least by Gwinner standards. E. G. and his
family discovered, however, that they couldn't do all the
work alone. They were particularly pleased when Uncle Ted
Melroe decided to rejoin them in 1949. He had had a
diverse and interesting career which included the operation
of restaurants in Stirum and Gwinner; an ill-fated Willys-
Overland dealership in Forman in which he had sold but
two cars in a year's time; a brief period as a Raleigh
Products representative; and war-time employment at the

Allen C. Holmstrom joined the company as a part-time welder, the only
one with the firm. A few years later
he was supervising more than 50
welders on the Melroe production
line.

Glenn Martin Bomber Company in Omaha, the Northern
Pump Company in Minneapolis and the Puget Sound Navy
Yard at Bremerton, Washington. In 1941 he had turned to
machinists' work after he had won $100 in a bank night
drawing at a Forman theater. The prize money had given
him the incentive to enroll in a 16-week course at the

Dunwoodie Institute in Minneapolis. After the war he returned to his hometown, worked for a year at the Gwinner Auto Machine Company and then served soup and sandwiches in his own eatery located in the former Gwinner State Bank building. The re-association with his older brother was to prove a mutually beneficial decision; he was ultimately to become the company's production superintendent, the tutor of numerous young machinists and a participant in the development of the firm's second major product: the Melroe Harroweeder.

Others began to join the ranks, too. Allen C. Holmstrom,

Most of the company's first employees were Gwinner area farmers or townspeople who started as part-time helpers and then stayed on the payroll permanently. (Top left) Clarence Hegle, (top right) Seavert Weeks, (bottom left) Art Hanson, (bottom right) Leon Maurer.

son of the local machine shop operator and baseball-playing chum of the younger Melroes, was typical of those outside the family who were associated with the enterprise from its beginning years. Al had worked for E. G. on the farm, and after World War II he became a welder on the Garrison Dam project. When construction took a winter hiatus, Al helped out in the Melroe plant. In 1950 he went to work full-time as the company's only welder; a few years later he was promoted to plant superintendent and had 55 welders under his direction.

Other Gwinner area farmers and townspeople—like Clarence O. Hegle, Roy Lecy, Kenneth Putman, Hal Coultas, Seavert Weeks, Art Hanson and Willie Truesdell—started mostly as part-time helpers and ended up on a year-around payroll. In 1947 the firm produced 150 pickups in the old schoolhouse; in 1948 the production rose to 500 in the new plant. A year later another 30x100 addition was constructed and 900 combine attachments came off the line. In 1950 a second story was added to the 60x100 factory, and 1,300 pickups were manufactured. Still, it was anything but a get-rich-quick proposition.

In 1949, for instance, the first extensive quality problems occurred. When just a few pickups were made by hand, E. G. could check them all individually; when a dozen or more were assembled each day, using materials supplied by other processors, the possibilities of malfunction were multiplied. That year the Melroe brothers dissipated their profits by making extensive field repairs because of faulty belting which stretched and caused spring steel teeth to operate ineffectively. The brothers themselves—by car and by truck—traveled to individual farms in a three-state area, personally restoring the recalcitrant machines. The experience had value, though: it taught the struggling manufacturers that quantity can be detrimental to quality if vigilant control is not maintained.

Another business facet the Melroes knew little about was advertising. Because E. G. had been an avid reader of *The*

Dakota Farmer through the years, he agreed to a small advertisement in that publication soon after the move from the schoolhouse. Basically, though, he was an inventor and a builder; merchandising and salesmanship were foreign to his nature, so it was incumbent upon his sons to step in where their father cared not to tread. In 1948 Rog and Irv loaded a pickup on a farm truck and drove to the South Dakota State Fair in Huron. They rented display space under a tree, leaned their attachment against it and waited for customers. Not many buyers materialized—but the brothers answered lots of questions.

E. G.'s youngest brother, Sig, played an important supporting role in the Melroe drama. He shared ownership with Ed of the 1927 Model P Case combine which he is shown preparing for Gwinner's golden anniversary parade in 1950.

John Maurer, long-time Gwinner mayor and former farm implement serviceman, recalled some of the earliest Melroe fair presentations with which he assisted. "Sometimes it took us four years to sell a farmer a pickup. The first year he'd look; the second year he'd be surprised to see us back again because we were such a small company. The third year he'd ask questions, and the fourth year he'd buy."

Maybe that's why the Melroes never gave up their

Sig made sure his infant grandson, Owen Dahl, was introduced to the hand-made pickup which two older generations of relatives knew most intimately.

original booth space in Huron, though their literature and displays became more sophisticated through the years and the number of their products increased!

One of the readers of the Melroe's first advertisement in *The Dakota Farmer* was a garrulous young ad man named Harold Flint. After World War II, Flint had established an agency in Fargo and was ever alert to find potential clients in North Dakota. Among the earliest beneficiaries of his talents was an imaginative restaurant cook who manufactured a later-day-cure-all called Lin-ox-ol. Flint's promotion genius almost resulted in the elixir becoming a run-away seller—until the Federal Food and Drug Administration officially frowned on the product's formula which consisted mostly of linseed oil. The agency survived, though, and in 1950 Harold Flint stopped in Gwinner while enroute through to another client meeting. He found the Melroes naive but quick to learn. They were unaware of the services provided by advertising agencies, but they were willing to listen to what Flint had to offer. As a result, two comple-

menting sets of talents were brought together, and in the
ensuing years the association was to prove profitable to
both parties.

Irv Melroe presented Harold Flint (right) with a metal sculpture of the
advertising executive on the occasion of the 20th anniversary of the latter's
agency in Fargo. John Clay of the Melroe advertising department created the
unusual caricature.

On December 27, 1950, Kari (Ellefson) Melroe—E. G.'s
mother—died in the Britton, South Dakota, hospital at the
age of 88. Her death marked the end of a family era which
spanned both the creation and development of the state of
North Dakota and the formative years of her son's manufacturing company. As an indomitable pioneering mother,
she, too, had contributed!

Chapter 10

Wheat Rust and
Nervous Bankers

The year 1951 was better than ever.

A contract was signed to furnish the Oliver Corporation with 300 pickups which would be included with new combines as standard equipment. The Gleaner Corporation of Independence, Missouri, ordered 50. Altogether the company produced more than 2,000 attachments for dealers throughout the Middle West and the grain-producing regions of Canada. On the West Coast, E. G.'s nimble-fingered apparatus found ready adaptation in the grass seed industry.

There were problems, though. The Korean War had brought federal restrictions and steel priorities. Being a new company, the Melroe organization had little influence in the scramble for steel stocks; furthermore, it was still without a solid credit rating because it was a relatively unknown firm in a "far off place." To get through the crisis, the Melroes bought scrap metal wherever they could find it, and personally hauled it into Minneapolis and Chicago where they sold it directly or traded it for new steel to use in the pickups.

Once again they had space problems, and a 60x100-foot warehouse was attached to the rear of the plant. By this time E. G. was no longer so reluctant to expand. He didn't even object much when his sons traded a combine and swather to Everett Stevens, their long-time neighbor, for a four-place Stinson airplane. Their reasoning, of course, was that they could give their dealers better service by air. In a way, Stevens had started it all by whisking Roger to Walhalla, North Dakota, for an emergency repair job. The trip went so well that Rog enrolled in a flight instruction course and became a pilot. Later, so did Irv and brother-in-law Gene Dahl.

As business growth continued, financing difficulties also increased. In 1952 the firm did three-quarters of a million dollars worth of business, all of which sounds like excellent progress—except that the company had outstripped its sources of capital. The farm operation had been able to back up a few thousand dollars worth of inventory, but the expanded manufacturing program required an altogether different approach. The rob-Peter-to-pay-Paul system was no longer feasible.

The first major crisis came in 1953 when a wheat rust epidemic struck North Dakota and spread over into South Dakota and the Canadian provinces of Saskatchewan and Alberta. The destructive fungus caused farmers to plow under vast acreages of grain—and as a direct result, hundreds of orders for Melroe pickups were cancelled. The unsold pickups were placed under lock-and-key by a warehouse financing company, a situation which was embarrassing not only to the Melroes but to the dozen or more full-time employees who had by then cast their lots with the family firm. It had been the family custom to hold business meetings around Mabel's kitchen table, and in true Scandinavian tradition, she kept the coffee pot ever-present. As the financial squeeze began to develop, there were more meetings and more coffee. More than once it was suggested that the doors be locked and the entire operation disbanded—but the Mollerud-Melroe tradition of overcoming obstacles prevailed, and it was decided to ride out the storm or sink in the attempt.

Almost in desperation, Les made a call on the Oliver Corporation. He explained his family's plight and asked if there was something the Oliver organization could do to help, since that firm had adopted the Melroe pickup as standard equipment on its combines. As a result, he got a cash-on-the-barrelhead order for $80,000, enough to pay off the most demanding creditors and to assure another season of production. The Oliver representatives swung a hard bargain, but they made it possible for the Melroe Manufacturing Company to stay alive.

But that was just the beginning of the pecuniary problems. The wheat rust debacle had destroyed the company's banking arrangements in the St. Paul area where the firm had been forced to seek credit when local sources had failed them. The Sargent County Bank of Forman was willing to advance money for the farm operation and to help the Melroe Implement Company (a local Massey-Harris dealership taken over in 1951 and operated by the family for about seven years), but the money demands of the manufacturing operation were just too much of a vault-full for the smaller bank to consider.

Other North Dakota lending institutions were equally reticent. A Fargo banker sent regrets, saying that the Melroe firm was too far away for his organization to serve. In Gwinner and Sargent County, individuals were investing in Toronto oil stocks and Florida land schemes, while the local company was approaching a financial crisis for want of working capital.

The situation came to a head over an order placed with the Reynolds Aluminum Company. It was evident to the family council that there was no way to pay for the materials—no matter how badly they were needed—so Rog called Minneapolis to cancel the shipment. The Reynolds representative in the Twin Cities was friendly and persuasive. His company wasn't worried about the Melroe credit, he said. "Take the aluminum and pay for it when you can," he insisted. Though the supplies were desperately required to maintain production schedules, Rog spelled out the blackness of the financial picture and told the metal supplier not to send the order. "Don't worry," was the reply. "The truck is already enroute, and I'm sure that something can be worked out."

The aluminum arrived, and apparently there was going to be no problem. That's when the call came from the Reynolds office in Chicago.

"Where is the money for the shipment?" the credit man wanted to know.

Rog explained his conversation with the representative in Minneapolis, pointing out that his firm was fresh out of capital and that he and his family could see no possible way out of quandry. "I'm sorry," said the caller, "but our representative had no authorization for extending credit. You'll either have to pay or we'll be forced to take some sort of action against you."

That instant marked one of the major turning points in the Melroe company's history!

There was a brief pause because Roger simply had nothing to say. Then the voice from Chicago went on: "In looking over your records, it seems to me that your

When the Melroe Company depended entirely upon its pickup production, financial stability was difficult to attain. Jerome Reiser was pictured on the assembly line.

company is an excellent risk; you show no credit defaults or other indications of unsound operation. Somebody should be willing to take a chance on you."

The Reynolds man suggested the First National Bank of Chicago and offered to make the necessary introductions if any of the Melroes would like to come to the Windy City. Needless to say, the company airplane was cranked up in a hurry, and Rog and Cliff headed for Illinois. Their interview was successful enough to bring two bank representatives to Gwinner, and the report of what they saw convinced the First National directors that the North Dakota firm should be on their lending list. The bank decision not only gave the Melroes a much-needed morale boost, but it meant that they could go forward and not back. They were, like the prophet of old, more appreciated in far away places!

By this time E. G. and his family partners could see that a one-product organization could be a worrisome arrangement, especially when the product was seasonal and dependent to a great degree on the whims of the weather and such agricultural vagaries as wheat rust epidemics. During the financial ups-and-downs, Ed had been working on an aluminum-slat draper for swathers. It was designed somewhat like a continuous venetian blind, and its purpose was to eliminate the continual shrinking and stretching of the canvas belting which was generally used for such purposes. The Melroe draper actually went into production briefly, enjoyed a fleeting moment of acceptance and was then withdrawn from the market because of manufacturing difficulties.

He and Cliff had another idea, though, and the two family inventors put their heads together for the good of the organization!

As good as it was, the Melroe pickup was a seasonal sales item subject to the whims of the weather and such agricultural vagaries as wheat rust. In 1953 cancelled orders created a financial crisis.

Chapter 11

A Monument to E.G.

Ed Melroe was a conservative in politics and business, but on the farm he tended to be more liberal, both in his actions and in his thinking. He experimented while others doggedly clung to old methods. Sometimes he got carried away in his exuberance, like the time he planned to go into the chicken business in a big way, only to get sidetracked in his coop-building program. A flock of heavy-laying Leghorns had the run of the farm, and for a time the Melroes lived in the middle of a giant daily Easter egg hunt. Everybody gathered eggs when they stumbled across them, and the two youngsters—Evelyn and Irv—had to wash and crate as many as 300 eggs a day.

111

E. G. was not a demanding taskmaster, but he liked to
see his sons and hired hands make haste in the fields. In his
estimation, tractors were not built to poke along on, and
the equipment they towed had to be designed to work
efficiently at the maximum speed. That's why he drove
behind harrows and other machinery to observe the action
on the ground or rode a tractor with a stop-watch to learn
what he could about engine timing and to speculate on
possible improvements.

Tooth harrows, or drags as they are sometimes called,
were of continual concern to E. G. They were vital to the
preparation of seed beds, but they were anything but
modern in their concept and design. The old Boss Harrow—consisting of little more than a frame of heavy
timbers with large railroad-type spikes driven through
them—might well have been conceived by an ancient farmer
just a few years into the Iron Age. It did the work but it
had many drawbacks: it was cumbersome and required two
or three men (or strong farm wives) to unload it from a
wagon or truck; weeds clung to the teeth and every now
and then the operator would have to stop and untangle the
creeping jenny or other matted vegetation; the teeth dulled
and lost their efficiency or they were broken and bent by
rocks; if the tractor went too fast, the harrow would rise
up out of the ground and fail to do its job; it tended to
"powder" the ground and aggravate wind erosion. The later
all-metal drags with replaceable teeth had the same general
deficiencies, though it was possible to keep the spikes sharp
if someone were everlastingly at the grindstone.

E. G. pondered these shortcomings, trying to develop
some new approach to an age-old farm operation. The
break-through came one day in 1952 when a sample box of
spring teeth arrived from the American Spring & Wire
Company. Ed and Cliff looked through the collection
which contained several steel teeth somewhat larger than
those used on the combine pickup. Father and son discussed the possibilities of a strong, but resilient wire spike

Brothers Ted and Ed Melroe worked endless hours in the development of the company's first commercial spring-tooth Harroweeder and fold-up drawbar.

for harrowing action—and the basic idea for a revolutionary agricultural tool was born.

Again there was a lengthy period of experimentation and development. At first E. G. fastened the spring teeth to sections of angle iron, and though the device wasn't as successful as he had hoped it would be, it at least gave him encouragement to continue the project. Not only was it apparent that he was on the right track, but his earliest models revealed several advantages he and Cliff hadn't even considered. The springiness of the teeth caused them to vibrate through the earth, dislodging shallow-rooted weeds while mulching the soil. The stirring action caused larger clumps of earth to come to the top, while the finer particles settled to the bottom; not only did this provide an ideal seed bed for most crops, but it appreciably reduced wind erosion by eliminating the powdery surface often created by conventional harrows.

Meanwhile, a second phase of the project was under concurrent development. From a logistics point of view, conventional harrows consisted of two general types: those which had to be hand-wrestled on and off truck beds each

E. G. on his 62nd birthday in 1954.

time they were moved from field to field, and the wide, one-piece models which could be transported on special running gear but which provided a frightful road-spanning traffic hazard on public byways. Through the years each time one of his hired men pulled a sprawling drag down one of the Bowen Township roads, E. G. could visualize a disastrous collision with its attendant miseries and lawsuits. He had long thought about a sectionalized fold-up harrow which could be loaded easily onto a cart no wider than a tractor. The new Melroe product, he decided, should be designed to solve the vexing transport problem, too.

So in the midst of the financial difficulties of the early fifties, he, his sons and brother Ted worked out the details of the Harroweeder (as it was to be officially labeled) and a drawbar which would serve as a carrier for the new agricultural tool. They discovered that proper tempering of the coil spring teeth was the key to success of the Harroweeder itself. If the wire spikes were not hard enough to resist wear and resilient enough to avoid breakage, the device simply wouldn't be practical. Patiently they built, tested, re-built and tested again, and just before the product of their labors was ready for its market debut, E. G.

became ill and was hospitalized in Minneapolis. His latest affliction was diagnosed as a gall bladder attack, and he submitted to surgery.

For 16 years he had suffered almost continual pain from his leg amputation. Periodically his heart problem returned, and his sons and other Melroe employees were ever alert to see that a nitroglycerine capsule was placed under his tongue when an attack occurred. He always bounced back, but this time was the solitary exception. On April 30, 1955—seven days after his 63rd birthday—he died from complications arising from the operation.

E. G. Melroe was an unusual man. His achievements, by historical standards, were not great, but in his station in life—as a North Dakota farmer, the father of a closely knit family and an inventor by impulse and necessity—he was amazingly successful. Politically, he never sought office, but he spoke his mind in old-fashioned American tradition on the Gwinner street corners. He was proud of his sons and his son-in-law for what they were accomplishing under the banner of the Melroe Manufacturing Company. The latter was to become a living, dynamic monument to E. G.'s memory, for without him, it never would have happened.

The day of his funeral—May 3 – was, as his daughter put it, "a day you wouldn't believe." A dust storm as bad or worse than those of the Dirty Thirties swirled across Sargent County. Street lights were turned on at mid-day. Bill Bruns, one of the honorary pallbearers, was so engulfed in the choking dust that he drove into a ditch on the way from Crete and never made it to the services. Flashlights were used to direct traffic at the church site. It was almost as if the specter of wind erosion had risen up in one final burst of defiance against a man whose ideas would soon be instrumental in curbing this vicious scourge so detrimental to North Dakota agriculture.

In spite of the weather, the Gustaf Adolf Lutheran Church in Gwinner was filled to overflowing. Many of the

mourners were individuals whom E. G. had helped through
one crisis or another; all of them were his friends. Among
the honorary pallbearers were Art Holmstrom, who had lost
his favorite machine shop visitor; Carl Nelson, Bill Jentz
and Everett Stevens, who recalled exciting winter trips to
the Southland with their wives and the Melroes; Harry
Wallace, Rub Johnson, Roy Cole, Sig Anderson, John
Maurer, A. E. Hillestad and Harry Spaulding, all of whom
reminisced silently about their many personal experiences
with E. G. Reverend Raymond B. Torgersen read from the
23rd Psalm, and finally the cortege made its eerie way
through the dust-laden haze to the Gwinner cemetery
where conditions were so bad that it was impossible to
complete customary grave-side rites.

Two days later, in its report of the funeral, the *Sargent
County News* eulogized Edward G. Melroe in a brief but
pointed remark: "He helped build the community in which
he lived by operating the only industry in the county—a
plant of which the entire state of North Dakota is proud."
As the ensuing years were to prove, it became a most
appropriate epitaph!

E. G. did not live to see the full realization of the
company he founded; he did, however, have the confidence
that his heirs were prepared to assume the responsibilities
of his dream. Though he had worked hard and experienced
an ample share of ups-and-downs, he certainly had not had
a totally drudgerous and humdrum life. He took time to
enjoy himself and made sure that his family did, too. Leon
Maurer, who was to become a Melroe Company official,
told how E. G. treated him and other younger men "almost
like sons," and even when they were driving across the
state to some important business meeting, it was not
unusual for Ed to turn off the road at some such place as
the sand hills north of Wyndmere and literally stuff himself
with wild raspberries. He was, as his son-in-law Gene Dahl
described him, "a truly genuine man."

His love of fine automobiles—dating way back to the
acquisition of his first sporty Briscoe—continued through-

A steel-tempering process developed by Cliff Melroe and Gordon Irwin, using World War II surplus furnaces, was responsible for the strength and resiliency of Harroweeder teeth.

Kenny Waloch and Bruce Stevens stacked completed Harroweeder sections.

E. G.'s genius—abetted by the ideas of his son Cliff, Eldon Nelson and others—ultimately resulted in a product which solved all of the basic problems of harrowing which the farmer-inventor had hoped to alleviate.

out his lifetime, and in his later years he was able to enjoy Cadillacs rather than re-built Flints. He did not flaunt his growing wealth, though his sons agreed that using a Cadillac for cross-country farm inspections and to burn stubble fields might somehow qualify as the height of luxury.

Life, of course, has a way of going on, and with E. G.'s passing, the Melroe brothers and Gene Dahl re-appraised the future of the business. The company was basically sound, but it was still a young, sprouting organization, subject to growing pains and unexpected problems. While Les, Rog and Irv concentrated on selling, and Gene devoted much of his time to the vital function of purchasing, it was up to Cliff to step into his father's shoes, both as official head of the company and as the mechanical watchdog and trouble-shooter. The Harroweeder was not functioning up to expectation, mostly because of teeth-tempering deficiencies. Cliff received little satisfaction from steel suppliers or metallurgists, so he resolved to find the answers himself. The company bought two surplus tempering furnaces which had been used to produce 20-millimeter shell casings during World War II. With the help of Gordon Irwin, a young engineering graduate, Cliff conducted the experimentation which ultimately resulted in the proper formulization: 18 minutes of 1,500 degree heat in a carbon-rich oven, rapid cooling to 120 degrees in an oil bath, then re-heating for 40 minutes at 800 degrees.

"The process sounds simple enough," said one of the company engineers, "but tempering steel is like baking bread—even with the same recipe, some women can and some women can't."

With the tooth problem solved, the Harroweeder became a much desired, much imitated farm implement, and the Melroe Manufacturing Company faced the future with another quality product of which E. G. would have been justifiably proud.

Oluf and Kari (Ellefson) Melroe

Mathilde and Ivar Petterson	Gina and Clarence Hansen	Edward G. and Mabel (Petterson)	Oscar and Esther (Edman)	* Sigurd and Myrtle (Petterson)	** Theodore and Marguerite (Bopp)
Lillian Florence	Norman Oluf	Lester Wedell	(no children)	Merriam Myrtle	Helen Carrie
Karyl Harold	Ardell Melbourne	Clifford Edward		Mardelle Lois	Eileen Louise
Ethel Imogene		Roger Theodore		Stanley Alan	
Caroline Selma		Evelyn Mabel		Lenore Marlys	
Mabel Louise		Irving Lowell		Sylvan Nels	
Edgar Lawrence					

* Sig's wife, Myrtle, died in 1949; in 1963 he was married to E. G.'s widow, Mabel, who was his first wife's sister.

** Ted's wife, Marguerite, died in 1937; in 1939 he was married to Mrs. Mae (LaBounty) Broomfield, a widow since 1934.

Chapter 12

A Family Affair

There were those who felt that when E. G. died, the Melroe organization would fall apart at the seams. They didn't count on the cohesiveness of the Scandinavian family nor the diverse talents of the sons Ed left behind. In 1955 Les, Cliff, Rog and Irv were no longer naive farm boys floundering in unfamiliar business circles; they were experienced industrialists who had already been through the financial wringer a few times.

They had done it the hard way! They knew what it was like to make cold sales calls and to spend long, sleepless hours in a truck cab, delivering pickups to far-flung dealers or hauling raw materials to Gwinner from Minneapolis,

E. G.'s dream was that his company would be a family affair; this team of four sons and a son-in-law fulfilled that goal. Seated (left to right): Clifford E. Melroe and Lester W. Melroe. Standing: Eugene R. Dahl, Irving L. Melroe and Roger T. Melroe.

Chicago or the major cities of the East. When they weren't tied up on some other mission for the company, they worked on the manufacturing line or they drove a tractor in the farm operation. They knew how to handle tools, and they were learning how to handle people. Consignments, sales meetings, advertising layouts and balance sheets had become part of their every-day language.

In 1954 Les, the oldest of the brothers, moved to Minneapolis to establish a sales branch and general service office for the company. In 1947 he had been married to Doris Carol Hegenes of that city and daughters Kristine Kay and Nancy Holly were born to them in 1949 and 1954, respectively.

Following E. G.'s death, Clifford, the second eldest, became president of the company. In 1946 he was married to Margaret Jean Taylor of nearby Milnor. Their first son, Bruce, was born in 1947, followed by David in 1948, Pamela in 1950 and Keith in 1951. The couple was divorced in 1966 and two years later Cliff was married to Pearl Shipley. A son, Charles, was born to them in 1968; by her earlier marriage, she had two children—Tracy, born in 1958, and Carrie, born in 1960.

Roger was the last of the brothers to establish a family. His bride in 1952 was Dorthea Cole of Cogswell in Sargent County. She had one son, Del, by a previous marriage; their daughter Vickie, was born in 1953, and a son, Robert, arrived two years later.

Irving's wife, the former Sylvia Hollan of Kulm, North Dakota, had taught school in Lisbon with Evelyn Melroe, who introduced the couple. They were married in 1948. A year later a daughter, Mary, was born, and in 1951 she was joined by a brother, Edward.

Gene and Evelyn Dahl added four more grandchildren to Ed's and Mabel's total: Howard, in 1949; Laura, 1950; Joan, 1952, and Brian, 1956.

In the earliest years of the company, the Melroe wives learned that they were also wedded to a combine pickup. They stapled canvas aprons in the plant or rode in truck cabs beside their husbands to keep them awake on long delivery runs. The ultimate success of the business became a family affair, which meant a great amount of sacrifice on everyone's part. Not that it was a dull, austere, all-work, no-fun existence, but it certainly was not a normal rural North Dakota pattern of life.

The wives also inherited Evelyn's childhood chore of delivering noon "dinner" and mid-morning and mid-afternoon lunches to the men when they were working on the farm. Their big problem was not the preparation of food, but finding their husbands on the widely scattered Melroe fields in Bowen and White Stone Hill townships. Each plot was known by the name of the owner from whom the land was leased or for some earlier proprietor who had sold out to E. G.

"We'll be in the Hanley quarter," the husbands would say when they left in the morning. Then it would be up to the wives to search their memories or their township maps to plan the logistics of their traveling food service. Sometimes the men would finish their work in one field sooner than they expected and move on to another maybe three or four miles away. On one occasion Sylvia and Doris decided to give husbands Irv and Les a special treat, so they rushed to the designated quarter with a carton of ice cream. Unfortunately, the men had departed for fields unknown, and an hour and a half later, the ladies were still driving around looking for their meandering farmers. Twice they had returned to town to replace the soupy dessert which failed to survive the North Dakota summer temperatures. It was, as Irv recalled, not the friendliest reunion when the wives finally found them.

Evelyn Melroe had grown up with that sort of thing. With four rambunctious brothers, she had learned to expect

With four athletic brothers, Evelyn Melroe admitted that she became a tomboy—by choice and by necessity.

the unexpected, and—almost as a matter of survival—she developed a few tomboy traits. It was imperative, for instance, that she could throw and catch a baseball. In time she became almost immune to their endless teasing. Mostly, though, she was her mother's chief assistant and companion on the somewhat remote farm dominated by men. Following her graduation from Gwinner high school, she attended North Dakota State University in Fargo where she received her degree in home economics in 1947.

That fall she signed a contract to teach in Lisbon, and just before Christmas, she and Eugene R. Dahl (whom she had known since they were in the first grade of the G. A. Lutheran Church Sunday School) were married. He was still finishing work on his degree at the University of North Dakota, so for a half year he commuted home to his bride on the weekends. After his graduation, both he and Evie accepted teaching assignments in the high school at Cava-

Nils Petterson was the first of the family legislators.

These family state legislators followed in Nils Petterson's footsteps: (seated) Henry (Hank) Petterson; (standing) Gene Dahl, Rog Melroe and Laurence (Laurie) Petterson.

lier, North Dakota. Pregnancy disrupted her career, and following the completion of his contract, they returned to Gwinner where Gene served for a year as teacher, coach and principal.

E. G. Melroe's vision of a family business included *all* his children, so in 1950 when the company gave indications that it truly had a future, he asked Gene to join the organization. When the latter agreed, E. G. had achieved one of his most important personal goals—the concomitance of his daughter and sons with their spouses in the mutual Melroe enterprise. It was, in effect, the fulfillment of Gunder and Maren Mollerud's dream one century removed.

E. G.'s passing generated a renewed dedication on the part of the family to make the company succeed. The financial hurdles were surmounted, the Harroweeder was introduced to a waiting market and in 1957 the firm's annual sales total climbed over the $1 million mark for the very first time.

The Melroe name began to create a stir within North Dakota business circles, and the salvation of Gwinner, a potential modern-day ghost town, was recognized as somewhat of a sociological miracle. Rog Melroe was elected to the state legislature in the footsteps of his maternal grandfather, Nils Petterson. (Gene Dahl was to achieve the same honor a decade later, as were Nils Petterson's sons, Henry and Laurence.) The company and its young officers had proved themselves to friends, kibitzers and skeptics alike.

The firm had become a two-product operation, solving to some degree the seasonal roller-coaster created by the combine pickup and its limited market. The Harroweeder made possible a better balanced, year-around production schedule, and by 1959 the firm's gross sales volume had topped the $2 million figure. Possibly the Melroe Manufacturing Company might have been content to level off at that comfortable plateau—had not Les stopped to have a cool drink at the home of one of his customers on a hot, humid day in mid-August of 1957.

Chapter 13

The Bobcat:
King of the Beasts of Burden

Anton Christianson, an implement dealer in Elbow Lake, Minnesota, took advantage of Les Melroe's visit to promote the talents of his two nephews who were blacksmith-machinists in a nearby town. By this time the Melroes were well enough known that they were regularly sought out by individuals with "brilliant ideas" which would surely revolutionize the agricultural industry. Usually these so-called brilliant ideas were totally impractical or they had been done before—but the Melroes kept looking and listening, not only because they could use new products for diversification, but because they remembered that they probably

129

wouldn't have been in business if the officials of the First
National Bank of Chicago and the Oliver Corporation
hadn't listened to them at critical times.

The day was oppressively hot, though, and Les was tired.
No doubt (he thought) Anton's nephews would have no
more to offer than the many other amateur inventors he
and his brothers had interviewed in the past. However, his
host had been both hospitable and persuasive, and when it
began to cool off later in the afternoon, Les agreed to drive
over to Rothsay, Minnesota, to meet Cyril and Louis
Keller. It was, as it turned out, one of the most important
decisions in the history of the Melroe firm.

In Rothsay, Cyril showed Les a small three-wheeled
self-propelled loader, so maneuverable that it could turn a
complete 360-degree circle in its own length. Les was
impressed; but because of the machine's limited size, he
was skeptical about its practical value.

The Bobcat, as it evolved, became a mover of cabbages (left), of pulp wood (above) and of almost every conceivable type of product.

Cyril and Louis had both worked in a foundry at Fergus Falls, Minnesota, and when the business appeared shaky, they pulled out and opened a blacksmith and machine shop in Rothsay. They had been in operation for several years when Eddie Valo, a local turkey farmer, came in with a problem. He wanted some sort of a machine to help him clean out his barns; the latter had so many upright poles that he couldn't find a mechanical device capable of zig-zagging among them.

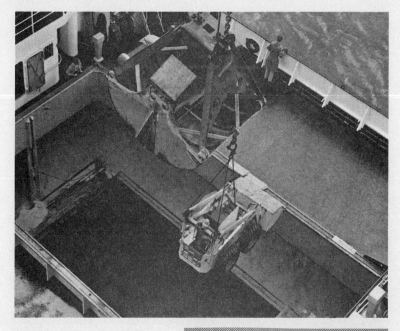

From the prairies of North Dakota the Melroe Bobcat was soon carried to all parts of the world to work on construction projects, in ships' holds and wherever the do-everything machine could be hoisted, driven or flown.

The Kellers agreed to try, though they didn't know exactly what approach to take at first. Just as E. G. Melroe had done on his earliest pickups, they scoured the junkyards, picking up a piece here and a piece there. Finally they put together a prototype model with two large drive wheels up front and a small caster wheel in the rear. The power was provided by a six-horse Kohler engine with a rope starter; the vehicle was steered by independent right and left levers, somewhat like a military tank. The fork tines of the hydraulically-operated scoop were made from bars taken from the windows of the old Rothsay jail. It was the only steel the Kellers could find which was hard enough to withstand the continual scooping and scraping.

The brothers built seven of the tri-wheelers, improving them as they went along, but in spite of considerable local interest in the Keller Loader, they were unable to push their idea much beyond the introductory stage. Les suggested that they take a machine to the Minnesota State Fair to test public reaction; then the Kellers were invited to Gwinner for a meeting with the other Melroe executives. The ultimate result was that the company bought the rights to the vehicle, and Louis and Cyril agreed to go on the Melroe payroll. The citizens of Rothsay offered to conduct a fund drive to keep the Kellers in their town, but the brothers were much like E. G.—they were builders, not promoters, and they recognized that their loader would never be successful without volume production and aggressive salesmanship. Rothsay's loss, therefore, was Gwinner's gain!

Once again no over-night miracle occurred. The Keller Loader as it was originally conceived had a limited potential, mostly because of its size, power and three-wheel design. Cliff Melroe especially (with his father's instincts for inventive modification) wanted to see a bigger, more versatile piece of machinery than the small turkey-barn cleaner. So for three years he and the Keller brothers worked on the conversion, adding weight, size, power and a fourth wheel. By 1960 all that remained of the original loader was the basic concept of the sealed-in-oil, lever-activated drive system—but the rugged, muscular mechanical jack-of-all-trades (still small enough to fit in the back of a pickup truck) was ready for a re-launching.

Then came the matter of a name!

The Melroe brothers wanted a euphonious monicker which would describe the capabilities of their new product while at the same time having forceful sales appeal. The company had engaged the services of Gould, Brown and Bickett, a Minneapolis advertising agency, to promote the re-designed loader, and while driving from the Twin Cities to Gwinner, Les Melroe and Lynn Bickett played a unique traveling game. Mile after mile they recited a litany-like list of possible names for the machine. None of them seemed to ring a bell, when almost as an afterthought, Lynn said, "How about Bobcat?"

Les liked the sound because it connoted a small but powerful animal, one with stamina and adaptability to its environment. In Gwinner the name was tried on Sylvan Melroe, at that time the company's advertising manager. He liked it, too, and he and Bickett developed the "tough, quick and agile" slogan which was to become a familiar phrase in Melroe circles. Later, at a staff conference, the Bobcat title was introduced, ultimately accepted and a new, exciting and financially rewarding chapter in the Melroe story was begun.

The Bobcat brought a major change to the organization. It was no longer a strictly agricultural manufacturing concern with a limit to its potential customers. With the debut of the do-everything loader, the company entered the industrial field with a product whose uses could range across the entire spectrum of a salesman's imagination. It took time, of course, to establish the production line, to sign up new dealerships and to readjust everyone's thinking to a divergent course of action.

In 1963, the Bobcat made its first substantial impact on the company's sales volume as the total surpassed $4¼ million. It was the beginning of a dynamic spiral, to $6½ million in 1964, $9 million in 1965, $12½ million in 1966, $16½ million in 1967 and to new pecuniary plateaus after that. Ironically, it was not E. G. Melroe's personal inventions which led the upward surge, but the results of his tutelage were evident in 1967 when his son, Cliff, was honored as North Dakota's Inventor of the Year for his contributions to the development of the combine pickup, the Harroweeder and the Bobcat. Because his family and the Melroe employees depended upon it, he, too, was an inventor by necessity!

In 1964 the first Bobcat to go overseas was shipped to Tutt Bryant, Ltd., in Sydney, Australia, the beginning of a vast new market—all served from the tiny town of Gwinner in southeastern North Dakota. A sales-and-service subsidiary—Melroe Ltd.—was established in Southampton, England, in 1966 to handle the growing demands for the Bobcat in Europe. That same year Bill Brooker of Atlanta, Georgia, became the first district representative of the company to produce over $1 million in sales in his area.

No wonder that William L. Guy, the governor of North Dakota could say:

> I know of no North Dakota corporation which, by its success, has brought so much pride to the people of our state. The growth of the Melroe Company has been dramatic proof that North Dakota can look forward to a broadening of its economy through manufacturing.

The evolution of the Bobcat was not without an occasional problem. Before a system of electrical stud welding was applied to the machine's body frame, someone in the field noticed that the big nuts and bolts on the left side of the loader came loose easier than those on the right. A visiting salesman—George LaFlamme of the Pudunk River

Electric welding (shown here with Ronald McFarland on the trigger) replaced bolted construction on the Bobcat when an unusual production problem cropped up (see text).

Equipment Sales Company in South Windsor, Connecticut—came up with the answer when he watched the Melroe assembly line in operation at the Gwinner plant.

"You've got a 200-pound man with a wrench on the right side and a 125-man on the left," observed George.

In time the Bobcat was fitted with posthole augers, rotary brushes, snowplows, back-hoes, grapple hooks, road scarifiers, pallet forks and pulp wood loaders. Masons, miners and merchant marine operators adapted it to multiple uses. The U. S. Army contracted for olive drab models instead of the familiar Bobcat white. In Plainfield, Iowa, Bill Roach unloaded a 50-ton boxcar full of ammonium nitrate in just one hour, one minute and 54.6 seconds with a Melroe Bobcat. Throughout the United States and numerous foreign countries, the oval decal with the bright red

Edgar (Bud) Petterson, the one-time baseball pitching star of the Melroe-Petterson clan, was photographed making an adjustment on the drive mechanism of an embryonic Bobcat.

lynx was appearing more and more regularly. Neither Cy nor Louis Keller had remotely envisioned such a national and international success; the Melroe brothers hadn't either!

The Bobcat, non-existent in E. G. Melroe's lifetime, had clawed its way into the family saga and promised an even brighter future for the ensuing years.

Mabel Melroe piloted a Bobcat at the 1965 ground-breaking for the new company office building. With her (left to right) were her children Cliff, Evelyn, Irv and Rog. Les was away from Gwinner at the time.

Chapter 14

People: The Plus Factor

In the earlier days the Melroe hiring policy was very simple. Irv would hand a prospective new employee a baseball glove, take him out to the parking lot and if he could catch, he had a job. Actually, that was more facetiousness than fact, but it did indicate the casual atmosphere of the family company when the work was still half farming, half manufacturing.

All of that has changed, however. The Melroe Company (the "Manufacturing" was dropped from the name in 1967) has become a highly efficient, conventionally operated business concern which would be equally at home in Detroit, Michigan; Pittsburgh, Pennsylvania; Trenton, New Jersey, or in one of the industrial parks of southern California.

The people probably wouldn't be, however!

141

Even when the employee roster topped 500 for the first time, an overwhelming majority of the workers were North Dakotans who had never left the state or who had returned "home" because they missed the elbow room, the crisp, smogless air and the relatively uncomplicated life on the prairie. Sociologists be damned! Gwinner didn't die; instead, in less than 20 years, it grew two and a half times its 1946 population.

The executive offices of the Melroe Company.

Crete, Stirum, Oakes, Milnor, Lisbon, Cogswell and other surrounding communities housed an increasing number of Melroe employees who could drive to Gwinner much easier than most big-city commuters could reach their bus stops or subway stations. The practice of hiring farmers part-time in the off-season was continued, not only because it provided the company with fill-in labor, but it gave the farmers of the area a secondary source of revenue.

Employee training techniques—as sophisticated as any in the nation—grew out of E. G.'s instructions to his sons and hired men on how to put the windrow pickup together. From the beginning, new workers were mostly unskilled, but they were generally North Dakota farm folks who knew how to weld, manipulate a wrench and overhaul a tractor. It didn't take long to familiarize them with a drill press, a steel cutter or a Harroweeder tooth kinker

When the need for more and more management person-nel began to develop, the Melroes looked internally and not afar. They had tried to import a few bright young men, but unless the latter had some background in Dakota living, they didn't stay long. So out of the ranks came loyal capable individuals like Allen C. and Lawrence (Bud) Holm-strom, Stanley G. Gunderson, cousins Ardell Hansen and Sylvan Melroe, Cy Keller (who remained on after his brother had retired), Leon Maurer and Gordon Trana. From Lisbon, North Dakota, came newspaper publisher Ferd Froeschle to serve as advertising manager. James W. John-ston, the company marketing director, grew up in Forest River. Graceville produced chief engineer James J. Bauer; service manager Thomas L. Stuart originated in Marmarth; purchasing agent Leonard E. Odde lived in Wahpeton before moving to Gwinner; Jack E. Johnson, the firm's production manager, went to General Motors from Oakes and then returned to his native state. Stan L. Oksness, a long-time Massey-Ferguson representative in Fargo, became the company's personnel manager.

(Top) Bruce Stevens maneuvers a brand new Bobcat. (Left) Harold Garoutte operates a sophisticated drill. (When he started, E. G. Melroe didn't even have electricity.)

(Top left) Ted Bauer, (top right) John Bock, (right) Stan Holmstrom work on the highly mechanized company assembly line, a far cry from the original hand work.

The pattern was typical, and it began to convince other North Dakotans that maybe the way to reverse the exodus of young native talent would be to encourage and abet local industry rather than to spend so much time and money trying to lure outside business firms with no roots in the state.

North Dakotans, for instance, had no trouble adjusting to the blizzard of March 3, 1966. The weather bureau called it the worst snowstorm of the century, and when it was over, it took 12 Bobcats, two Caterpillar dozers, almost two dozen workers and some 1,000 man-hours to clean the company streets and yards so operations could get back to normal. While the blizzard raged, 20 employees were stranded in the plant—so they worked out a shift arrangement, took turns sleeping on the conference room floor in the new ultra-modern office building and then did what they could to keep production schedules from falling too far behind. Nearby residents burrowed through the drifts to bring in hot dishes and sandwiches, and from Thursday afternoon until mid-day on Saturday the men consumed 36 gallons of coffee. It was the kind of old-fashioned tenacity which Ed Melroe would have appreciated!

For two decades the company officialdom consisted only of family members. Then in 1967 Robert N. Spolum, a native of Aberdeen, South Dakota, and Melroe controller for the preceding four years, was named vice-president for administration. It marked a milestone in the firm's management structure and demonstrated an awareness that there were more key bases to cover than Ed and Mabel had made arrangements for with four sons and a daughter.

Meanwhile, Gwinner, too, had prospered through the association. Not only had the once-dwindling population trend been reversed, but during Cliff Melroe's term as mayor, the town had begun a million-dollar streets, sewers and lighting program. Civic adrenaline had begun to flow again as new housing, a bowling alley, a motel, a branch bank, a supper club and the lighted Bobcat softball field

The Gwinner "International" Airport is within walking distance of the Melroe factory and is used extensively by company officers, customers, suppliers and salesmen flying in and out of the Sargent County town. Shown with one of the firm's planes are (left to right): Irv Melroe, Rog Melroe, brother-in-law Gene Dahl and Les Melroe. All but Les are licensed pilots.

were added to the local real estate. Gwinner "International" Airport—so named because of the number of foreign visitors flying in and out of the pasture-like strip just four blocks from the company plant—has developed into a valuable asset to the tiny town which was once difficult to get to and harder still to get away from.

It would be unrealistic to believe that a dynamic organization like the Melroe Company wouldn't ruffle an occasional feather or step on a sensitive toe now and then. The *Ransom County Gazette* of Lisbon editorialized on March 16, 1967:

> Melroe has had many small businessmen cussing it for picking off workmen and hired hands of all kinds. In this respect the firm has been hard on Lisbon, Oakes and nearby small towns. The same businessmen, some of them at least, have been grateful for the new business created by a larger Melroe work force in the area...The net result, very likely, has been economic prosperity to fill the gaps left by a continuing downward trend of the farm population. Huge progress? Maybe not, but at least the wheels of industry nearby have helped to maintain an even keel.

This was Gwinner's way of expressing its appreciation to the Melroe Company for civic favors.

The company has tried diligently not to throw its weight around, though it has been difficult to avoid on occasion. Not everybody in Gwinner works for the Melroes—and some are quick to announce that they don't. The company's $3½ million annual payroll has an obvious effect on the local economy, however, and both old and new businesses in the community have benefited from it. Some individuals have maintained their independence while working out mutually helpful arrangements with the Melroe

By 1964, when this picture was taken, the Melroe factory (left center) was already a dominant part of the Gwinner real estate. New housing began to crop up on the southern and eastern outskirts, and the once-dwindling village did a population about-face. This aerial photograph, though, depicts graphically the prairie isolation of North Dakota's unusual manufacturing center.

firm. Murray Heath, a Gwinner service station operator, for instance, became a sub-contractor, mounting tires on Bobcats and farm equipment. Melroe's ever-growing transportation needs has made it possible for William L. Huebner to develop a sizable terminal to service the truck fleet he leases to the company. The spirit of "neighboring," so vital in Oluf Melroe's day, is not entirely dead, though admittedly it has more commercial overtones.

Gwinner is not utopian by an means—but hardy, agriculturally-minded citizens kept it alive during the tough

The growth of the Melroe Company can be traced by this aerial view of the factory site. Gwinner's Main Street is at the far right.

times so it could ultimately enjoy some of the fruits of the Melroe successes. After all, it was the people—not buildings, or available raw materials, or ready markets—which kept E. G. and his family in the off-trail Sargent County town. Maybe they felt like the editor of *The Prairie Press* who wrote on February 9, 1933, in the depths of the Great Depression:

> It isn't the age of a town that makes it grow. It's the spirit of the people in it.

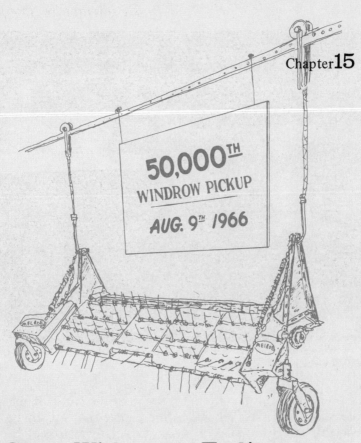

Chapter 15

50,000TH
WINDROW PICKUP
AUG. 9TH 1966

A Story Without an Ending

In 1966 Eldon Nelson, an inventive farmer from Clinton, Minnesota, showed up in Gwinner with a device he called the "Harrow-Matic" drag cart. The Melroe Company acquired his patent and, with a few modifications, introduced it as the Melroe Hydraulic Harroweeder. It eliminated the last bit of manual wrestling involved in that particular agricultural operation.

That year Melroe was responsible for a substantial majority of the spring-tooth harrow sections sold in the U. S. The firm also produced its 50,000th windrow pickup, thus giving it undisputed leadership in that product, too. In

151

Rog, Cliff, Les and Irv Melroe recalled the long years of development leading up to this milestone achievement: the production of the 50,000th Windrow Pickup.

Ed Reiten (left), shown receiving the 1965 Supplier-of-the-Year award from Cliff Melroe, had almost a quarter-of-a-century association with E. G. and the Gwinner firm before he sold his Cooperstown manufacturing company and its products to the Melroes in 1967.

The Reiten Manufacturing Company in Cooperstown, North Dakota, with a history dating back to 1938, became part of the Melroe organization in 1967. (Below) The Melroe brothers and other company officials welcomed the Reiten employees into the new fold following the change-over.

The Melroe brothers have never been able to get farming completely out of their systems. (Below) The original Oluf Melroe homestead 80 years after the claim was filed.

1967 Ed Reiten, a Cooperstown, North Dakota, machinist-manufacturer who had been producing component parts for E. G. as far back as 1943, sold his successful company to the Melroe organization. Reiten had developed a so-called trip-beam plow designed especially for work in rocky fields (when an individual plow share hits a stone, it automatically springs clear to let the obstacle pass by and then returns to its normal operating position). The plow and other Reiten products were added to the Melroe line to increase further its diversification.

As this book is being written, there may be another Eldon Nelson, an Ed Reiten, a Cy or Louis Keller knocking on the Melroe door in Gwinner. The company's research and development team—considerably larger than the firm's original working force—may unveil a revolutionary new farm tool. Cliff Melroe himself—or one of the other brothers, for that matter—may find a moment for mechanical creativity and add an entirely different outlook to the organization's future.

That's why this story cannot have an ending. By big-industry standards, the Melroe Company is still young, exuberant and as potentially versatile as its unbeatable Bobcat. There may be a new chapter tomorrow . . . and another the day after that . . . and the day after that!

Meanwhile, the family farm operation still goes on. The brothers enjoy an occasional tractor session, and Uncle Sig—E. G.'s brother—spends many hours on the original homestead where he raises registered Shorthorn cattle, just as Oluf Melroe did before him. Also on the farm is the old 1927 Case Model P combine, the unknowing catalyst of the entire saga. In 1963 Mabel Melroe, Ed's widow, married Sig, whose first wife, Myrtle Petterson (Mabel's sister), had died in 1949. The wedding was symbolic of the close relationship which ran—like an invisible but ever-present thread—through the length of the unusual family story.

This, then, is merely the end of the beginning!

Acknowledgments

Nothing adds to a writer's personal indebtedness like the production of a book. In this case, without the cooperation and talents of dozens of other individuals, the Melroe story could never have been compiled in this form.

First of all, I am most appreciative of the time and reminiscences offered me by the members of the Melroe and Petterson families so intimately intertwined in this saga and who are mentioned elsewhere in the volume. I'm including, of course, the cousins, double-cousins, nieces, in-laws and other relatives—like Mary Melroe, Ardell Hansen, Sylvan Melroe, Kathy Hartness and Carrie Bentson— who were quick to help when the project became known to them. From Norway, Theodor Mollerud sent a family tree and the lore of past generations.

I am especially grateful to Ferd Froeschle, advertising manager of the Melroe Company who provided logistics support and a vast store of information about the firm, the community and an unrelated topic of conversation called leafy spurge. His secretary, Dianna Bentson, was of continual help and warned of her current mood by alternating pictures of General Custer (a loser) and Sitting Bull (a winner) over her desk. Harold Flint, Fargo, North Dakota, advertising executive, traced for me the development of the organization as he saw it and introduced me to Lin-ox-ol and Gunderson flu.

In my estimation, L. T. (Vern) Laustsen has won the publisher-of-the year award for his generous assistance and encouragement. My thanks go also to Lew Campopiano of North Plains Press for both his patience and ability in overcoming the problems of production. Credit for cover design goes to Lowell Hanson, cover painting to Eugene Christopherson and for chapter illustrations to Jim Pollock. My continuing gratitude, of course, was merited once again

by my wife, Phyllis, who played her usual role of editorial
helpmeet and goader-first-class as deadline time approached.

There were many, many more—some of whom are listed
below. To them and those I may have inadvertently
overlooked, I offer my sincerest appreciation.

R.F.K.

Richard C. Crockett, Greater North Dakota Association
William M. Dreier
Lorix Halin
Mrs. Elvida Halin
Allen C. Holmstrom
Lawrence (Bud) Holmstrom
Mrs. Martha Holmstrom
Cecil Jahraus, *Ransom County Gazette*
Ernest Johnson
Cyril Keller
Mrs. Violet Kjelland
Carleton J. Likness, *Sargent County Teller*
Mrs. Colleen Majors, North Dakota State Historical Society
John Maurer
Leon Maurer
N. D. Nelson
Stan L. Oksness
Robert N. Spolum
Everett and Frances Stevens
Dale Webb

Index

Because the Melroes—four generations of them—are so intimately involved in this story and appear continually throughout the book, their names, and those of their spouses and children, have been excluded from this index. So, too, have been references to Gwinner, Sargent County, the Melroe Company, its products and other oft-repeated elements of the saga.

158